SING, O BARREN ONE

SOCIETY OF BIBLICAL LITERATURE

DISSERTATION SERIES
J. J. M. Roberts, Old Testament Editor
Charles Talbert, New Testament Editor

Number 91

SING, O BARREN ONE

by
Mary Callaway

Mary Callaway

SING, O BARREN ONE
A Study in Comparative Midrash

Scholars Press
Atlanta, Georgia

SING, O BARREN ONE
A Study in Comparative Midrash

Mary Callaway

Ph.D., 1979
Columbia University

Advisors:
James A. Sanders
George M. Landes

© 1986
Society of Biblical Literature

Library of Congress Cataloging-in-Publication Data

Callaway, Mary.
  Sing, O barren one.

  (Dissertation series / Society of Biblical
Literature ; no. 91)
  Bibliography: p.
  1. Women in the Bible. 2. Women in rabbinical
literature. 3. Childlessness in the Bible.
4. Childlessness in rabbinical literature. 5. Midrash.
6. Bible. O.T. Samuel, 1st II, 1–10—Criticism,
interpretation, etc., Jewish. I. Title. II. Series:
Dissertation series (Society of Biblical Literature) ;
no. 91.
BS680.W7C34 1986   220.9′2   86-15554
ISBN 0-89130-994-2 (alk. paper)
ISBN 0-89130-995-0 (pbk. : alk. paper)

Printed in the United States of America

לצביי

To Jamie, my gazelle

Contents

ACKNOWLEDGMENTS ix
ABBREVIATIONS xi

INTRODUCTION 1
    Midrash 5

Chapter

1. THE MATRIARCHS IN GENESIS 13
    The Social Context 13
    The Patriarchal Narratives 18
    The Function of the Motif 32
    The Yahwist's Methods 33

2. HANNAH 35
    The Function of the Motif 56
    The Methods of the Editor 57

3. SING, O BARREN ONE 59
    The Function of the Tradition
      in Second Isaiah 70
    Prophetic Hermeneutics 71

4. JERUSALEM OUR MOTHER 73
    The Feminine in Israelite Theology 73
    Zion as Mother in Isaiah 56-66 77
    The Function of the Image 80

  Jerusalem as Mother in the Book of Baruch 81
  Jerusalem as Mother in 4 Ezra 83
  Conclusions 89

5. SPIRITUAL CONCEPTION 91

  The Idea of Spiritual Barrenness 91
  Philo and the "Spiritual Conception"
   of Isaac 94
  Spiritual Conception in Luke's Infancy
   Narrative 100
  Sarah and Jerusalem in Gal 4:21-31 107
  The Relation between Paul's Sarah
   and Luke's Mary 113

6. THE MOTHERS AND THE RABBIS 115

  The Motif of the Seven Barren Women 117
  The Motif of Answered Prayer 123
  The Motif of Raising Up the Lowly 130
  The Motif of the World to Come 135
  Conclusions 137

EPILOGUE 141

BIBLIOGRAPHY 143

INDEX 153

Acknowledgments

This work was completed in 1978, with the assistance and support of many people. My gratitude to all who helped, those named and those unnamed, will be most clearly shown not here, but in my efforts to do for my students what so many have graciously done for me.

I am especially grateful to James A. Sanders, who set me on the path of Torah studies, disciplining me in its rigors, and encouraging me on the way. By inviting participation in his own work on comparative midrash, he allows his students to see a scholar at work, while leading them to develop their own abilities. His own deep insights into the formation of biblical traditions have shaped my approach to Scripture, and his respect for his students has been my most important preparation for teaching.

Special thanks to George M. Landes, whose meticulous attention to detail and care with the biblical text provided a model of scholarship.

To Robert Sacks, of St. John's College, Annapolis, to Merrill Miller and to Lloyd Bailey, and to many rabbinical students and professors at the Jewish Theological Seminary, I owe thanks for introducing me to rabbinic exegesis and for helping me to understand the divine sense of humor.

Finally, I thank my family, who in their own way have deepened my knowledge of Torah and, with their own wonderful pedagogy, my understanding of grace. To Jamie, for loving extravagantly and for never doubting, to Daniel, who was born in the midst of this work, and to Hannah, who bears the name, I gratefully acknowledge the support that made this work possible.

Abbreviations

Rabbinic Texts

'Ag.Ber.	Bereshith Aggadah
Pesiq. Rab Kah.	Pesikta de Rab Kahana
Gen. Rab.	Genesis Rabbah
Cant. Rab.	Canticles Rabbah
Pesiq. R.	Pesikta Rabbati
B. Meṣ.	Baba Metzia
Yal.	Yalkut Shimoni

ANQ	Andover Newton Quarterly
BA	Biblical Archaeologist
Bib	Biblica
BZ	Biblische Zeitschrift
CBQ	Catholic Biblical Quarterly
DBSup	Dictionnaire de la Bible. Supplément
GKC	Gesenius' Hebrew Grammar, ed. E. Kautzsch, tr. A. E. Cowley
IDBSup	Supplementary volume to IDB
Int	Interpretation
JAAR	Journal of the American Academy of Religion
JBL	Journal of Biblical Literature
JBR	Journal of Bible and Religion
JJS	Journal of Jewish Studies
NRT	La nouvelle revue théologique (NRTh)
RSO	Rivista degli studi orientali

RSR	*Recherches de science religieuse*
SBLASP	Society of Biblical Literature Abstracts and Seminar Papers
USQR	*Union Seminary Quarterly Review*
VT	*Vetus Testamentum*
ZAW	*Zeitschrift für die alttestamentliche Wissenschaft*

Introduction

One of the exciting issues in biblical studies today is the question of how the literature of Israel was sifted and culled so that a small portion was preserved and became authoritative or "canonical." What factors determined that certain traditions would be repeated and preserved while others would be forgotten and would vanish? The idea that the canonical books were decided by councils handing down their decisions to the faithful has given way to the concept of a *process* by which the books took shape and became authoritative.[1]

The ability to adapt old material to new purposes was always one of the special abilities of Israel's theologians. Most of the central biblical motifs—covenant, the kingship of God, the cycle of festivals—were adapted from the religions of Israel's neighbors. The biblical writers were masters at reinterpreting mythological polytheistic traditions into the service of Israelite monotheism.

The creative use of old traditions is evident in the prophetic writings, where the way in which the Torah traditions is interpreted in the present becomes one of the central concerns. Indeed, the differences in the way

---

[1] Some of the more recent important works which probe the nature of this process are Jack P. Lewis, "What Do We Mean By Jabneh?" *JBR* 32 (1964) 125-32; Morton Smith, *Palestinian Parties and Politics That Shaped the Old Testament* (New York: Columbia University, 1971); J. A. Sanders, *Torah and Canon* (Philadelphia: Fortress, 1972); and "Adaptable for Life: The Nature and Function of Canon," *Magnalia Dei: The Mighty Acts of God* (eds. F. M. Cross, W. E. Lemke and P. D. Miller; Garden City: Doubleday, 1976) 531-60; "Torah," *IDBSup* (Nashville: Abingdon, 1976) 909-911; and Joseph Blenkinsopp, *Prophecy and Canon* (Notre Dame: University of Notre Dame, 1977).

these traditions were interpreted was one of the chief differences between the "true" and "false" prophets of Israel.² One of the main aims of the present study is to show how this process of interpretation, which characterized Israel from her beginning, was one of the formative factors in the canonization of the Scriptures. The intimate relationship between canonization and interpretation and the relative nature of canonization is intimated by the Jewish tradition of the written Torah and the oral Torah. The interpretative traditions are the תורה שבעל פה; they too are Torah and they too have authority in the religious community.

The relation between the process of interpretation which led to canonization and the process of interpretation which produced the midrashic works of the Second Temple period is clear when we look at the presuppositions of both. In both cases the prerequisites are (1) a tradition which is known and is in some way authoritative; (2) a means of interpreting that tradition, i.e., a set of hermeneutical principles; (3) a community which has questions and concerns that can be addressed by the tradition.

In his work on the canonical process, J. A. Sanders has shown that it is the two poles of stability and adaptability which characterize canon.³ To become canonical a tradition must have stability; that is, it must be known and have some authority (although not necessarily a formal authority). But it must also have adaptability; it must be able to function in contexts other than its original one.⁴ Sanders' work has illustrated how reflection on the Patriarchal traditions in the context of the Exile resulted in canonization. The stories were ancient, well known and stable;

---

²See J. A. Sanders, "Hermeneutics in True and False Prophecy," *Canon and Authority* (eds. G. W. Coats and B. O. Long; Philadelphia: Fortress, 1977) 21-41.

³In addition to the works cited in n. 1, see "Biblical Criticism and the Bible as Canon," *USQR* 32 (1977) 157-165; "From Isaiah 61 to Luke 4," *Christianity, Judaism and Other Greco-Roman Cults* (ed. Jacob Neusner; Leiden: Brill, 1975) 75-106.

⁴This dual nature of the biblical materials was described in 1959 by Joseph L. Blau as characteristic of religion: "Not least of the elements of paradox that enter into the very nature of religion is the necessity that lies upon it, in its organized and institutionalized forms, to change while both seeming changeless and protesting its changelessness." For Blau, it is the use of hermeneutics that has been the most characteristic method for adapting Judaism to its changed surroundings. See his "Tradition and Innovation," *Essays on Jewish Life and Thought* (eds. Blau, Friedman, Hertzberg and Mendelsohn; New York: Columbia University, 1959) 95-104.

Introduction 3

they therefore had authority with the people. But they were also adaptable; they could take on new dimensions and significance in a new context and could provide answers to the most vital questions which the exiled people were asking. It is the questions of identity and life style which the traditions must be able to address, the questions: "Who are we and what are we to do?" The traditions which could speak to those concerns, through *muthos* (story) and *ethos* (law) were the traditions which were preserved and studied.[5]

In early Judaism and Christianity the process of searching the Scriptures proceeded on the same basis as that by which the Judahites in the Exile "searched" their Bronze Age traditions and the words of their prophets to answer their questions. The same stability and adaptability which allowed the ancient traditions to speak with authority in the new context of the Exile also allowed them to speak to many different contexts in the Second Temple period. In his study of early Jewish hermeneutic Daniel Patte gives the two functions of Scripture in "classical" Judaism: to give the community its identity as the chosen people with the vocation of sanctifying the Name and to provide a set of criteria which would enable the community to fulfill its vocation.[6] The functions of Scripture are clearly seen in the products of studying Scripture: haggadah and halakah.

It is the relation between the process of interpretation which led ultimately to the Canon and the process of interpretation that characterized Second Temple Judaism which I will explore in the following pages. By tracing the ways in which one specific tradition—the stories of the barren matriarchs—functions in different contexts, I shall demonstrate in a specific way the relation between the formation of the Scriptures and the later interpretation of them.

My method is purposely specific rather than general. It is not the time in the study of early Jewish literature for more comprehensive surveys or for new syntheses. The data simply are not in yet. What is needed, rather, are close and careful studies of individual traditions and their midrashic development in Second Temple Judaism.[7] By following the development of

---

[5]For discussion of the terms see "Adaptable for Life," cited in n. 1, especially section III.

[6]Daniel Patte, *Early Jewish Hermeneutic in Palestine* (Missoula: Scholars, 1975) 122-25. Patte's term "classical Judaism" is anachronistic; however, his analysis is useful.

[7]See, for example, Merrill P. Miller, "Targum, Midrash and the Use of the Old Testament in the New Testament," *JJS* 2 (1971) 29-82, esp. 75-76, and Anthony J. Saldarini in a review of Patte's book, *JBL* 96 (1977) 622.

one tradition, we can begin to see the kinds of contexts in which it occurred, the functions which it had and the literary genres in which it became embedded. In time the results of these studies will provide the data for a new understanding of early Jewish exegesis and for a new synthesis. The old models are no longer useful, but it is too soon for new ones. The goal of this study is to provide one solid brick for the edifice which will one day be constructed.

The rabbis, the evangelists and the other Jewish interpreters not only adapted the biblical motif of the barren matriarchs; they also tended to adopt the hermeneutical principles which the biblical authors used. Their interpretations were not artificial but had some basis in the interpretive tradition of the biblical text. The ways in which the biblical authors adapted traditions to a new context provided Jewish exegetes of the Second Temple period with some principles of interpretation. In the barren matriarch traditions and in their midrashic developments, at least, there is striking continuity between the Scriptures and the Midrashim.

However, there is also discontinuity between the function of the tradition in the biblical texts and in the midrashic texts of the Second Temple period. In this discontinuity we can begin to discover some of the unique aspects of Jewish exegesis. In what contexts did the barren matriarch tradition function in ways not found in the Bible?

I have chosen the stories of the barren matriarchs as the focus of this study in comparative midrash for three reasons. First, it is a tradition which has not been seriously studied, but which is usually assumed to be a motif of folklore. Why were so many of the important mothers in the Hebrew Bible barren before they had children? Are there literary and traditio-historical links between them? What is the relation between "Sarah our mother" and "Jerusalem the mother of us all?"

Second, it is a tradition which was interpreted in the tenth century B.C.E., the sixth century B.C.E., the second century B.C.E., the first century C.E., and later. Because it was able to function in so many different contexts, both in biblical times and afterwards, it provides a lens with which to focus on the relationship between stability and adaptability. The barren matriarch tradition is particularly interesting because of the way in which it became significant in the two heirs of the religion of Israel. In the first century C.E., the barren woman motif was central in early Christian reflection on the origins of Jesus, and also in rabbinic Jewish reflection on the nature of God's activity. What was it about this tradition that made it so durable in Israel? Why was it able to function in so many different situations? What did those barren women mean to the communities of the faithful in such diverse times and situations?

Finally, the tradition of the barren matriarchs provides a feminine image in a religious context for which such imagery was rare. The tradition becomes more and more important in the Second Temple period and it appears to be cumulative; new uses of the tradition do not go back to the sources only, but build on the interpretations which had grown up around it and, apparently, become authoritative. Were the feminine dimensions of the traditions related to its growing popularity and use? How would such a feminine tradition have been heard in the various contexts in which it appeared? While this question is only a sub-plot of our story, it is related to the main purpose of understanding how the tradition functioned in various contexts.

MIDRASH

We shall not attempt to define the term midrash, as that would not be the most fruitful way to clarify such a complex and rich activity.[8] A more helpful approach is to point out the origins and characteristics of midrash in order to understand something of its nature. It must be said at the outset that midrash is a peculiarly Jewish activity. It is not simply an exegetical method; it is rather a way of thinking.

Midrash is first of all a way of interpreting Scripture in the context of one's life and interpreting life in the context of Scripture. It presupposes a view of Scripture which is dynamic rather than static, in which Scripture is read as the living word of a living God which is addressed to a community living in the present.

In his review of Addison Wright's *The Literary Genre Midrash*, Roger le Déaut articulates how this view of Scripture is the basis of midrash:

> The term *midrash* expresses the conviction that the ultimate answer is to be found in searching the Scriptures, where it will be revealed to whoever knows how to search; *midrash* signifies the magnetization which it works on the Jewish soul, this tropism of religious thought under the influence of the revealed Word. Scripture is a living thing; it has never become a mummy: a living breath which permeates and quickens all of life emanates from it. Midrashic instruction can be compared with the manna with which Moses nourished

---

[8]For historical background, as well as discussion of the problems of a definition, see Merrill Miller's article, "Midrash" in the *IDBSup* (Nashville: Abingdon, 1976) 593-597.

Israel in the desert (Targum to Eccl. 12:11). If it is impossible to define midrash, it is because it has known an immense popularity, as a part of Jewish *life* and as a part of that sphere of the existential which refuses to be conceptualized, where it is first of all the response to the question: What does Scripture want to say for the life of today? And no effort is spared—even at the price of methods which are strange to us—to allow it to make its response.[9]

Scripture, then, is used to make sense out of contemporary events and to answer the question "how shall we live?" in times of crisis.[10] Wright defines midrash as "a literature about a literature. A midrash is a work that attempts to make a text of Scripture understandable, useful, and relevant for a later generation. It is the text of Scripture which is the point of departure, and it is for the sake of the text that the midrash exists."[11] The problem with this definition is that it tips the delicate balance which is at the heart of midrash: the relation between Scripture and the life of the community. Le Déaut, using Max Kadushin's word, argues that the biblical text is rather "very often little more than a stimulus for a composition which is developed in complete independence of it."[12] Kadushin makes an important observation in this regard:

> The biblical texts, then, were not employed simply as pegs for rabbinic ideas that had already been thought out. The texts played a rôle in the development of the rabbinic ideas; the ideas are midrashim, interpretations of the texts.[13]

---

[9] "Apropos A Definition of Midrash," *Int* 25 (1971) 270. Translated from the French in *Bib* 50 (1969) 395-413 by the present writer.

[10] The phrase is from Ezek 33:10 and is used by Sanders in "Adaptable for Life," section VIII.

[11] *The Literary Genre Midrash* (Staten Island: Alba House, 1967) 74. Wright's book, together with Le Déaut's review, are important in the discussion of the "broad" and the "narrow" definitions of midrash. In the *IDBSup* article cited above, Merrill Miller concludes that there is no satisfactory way to solve the problem of definition, at least for the present. In our study of the barren matriarch traditions we hope to contribute to the discussion of the broad and the narrow definitions by showing how the midrashim (in the narrow sense) come out of a very long process of midrashic interpretation (in the broad sense).

[12] *Apropos* 274.

[13] *The Rabbinic Mind* (New York: Bloch, 1972) 114-115.

Kadushin's point underlines the nature of midrash as an activity, a creative process through which the rabbis arrived at a new perception about the world. By saying that Scripture is like the manna, the rabbis were suggesting that it nourishes, sustains and enlivens the people of God. It is difficult to maintain that most midrashim exist "for the benefit of the original text"[14] when they move so far from the plain meaning of the text, and even, as Le Déaut points out, interpret passages in contradiction to their plain meaning. The rabbis did not search the word of God for the benefit of the text, but rather for the benefit of the people of God.

While midrash can be legitimately called a Jewish activity, it is nonetheless rooted in the biblical literature. Renée Bloch, in her now classic article on midrash,[15] traces the development of midrash from its origins to post-exilic times, when the Torah emerged as the one common possession of the Jews. At that time, those who sought the word of the Lord no longer visited a seer or a prophet, for the age of prophecy was past, but they searched the Torah. The prophets and sages of the exile incorporated midrashic procedures into their works, as Bloch shows, e.g., in Ezekiel 16, Chronicles, 3 Isaiah, and the post-exilic Psalms.[16]

Brevard Childs has added evidence of the biblical roots of midrash in his article, "Midrash and the OT."[17] He proposed that the relation between midrash and the OT can best be determined by clarifying the form and function of various exegetical activities within the Bible which are analogous to those of classical rabbinic midrash. He finds three such exegetical activities in the OT: citation of Scripture (3 Isaiah cites 2 Isaiah, 2 Chr 5:2 cites Jer 29:14); harmonization of diverse texts (seen especially in Chronicles); and the establishment of a new context for a text, as for example the way in which the superscriptions of many of the Psalms set them in the context of the historical life of David.

---

[14] *Midrash* 74.
[15] "Midrash," *DBSup* 5 (1957) cols. 1263-81, or see the English translation made by the present writer in *Approaches to Ancient Judaism: Theory and Practice* (ed. William S. Green; Missoula: Scholars, 1978) 29-53.
[16] For a more recent study of how reflection on ancient traditions affected the shape of the Torah, see J. A. Sanders, "Torah" in *IDBSup* (Nashville: Abingdon, 1976) 909-911.
[17] *Understanding the Sacred Text* (ed. John Reumann; Philadelphia: Fortress, 1972) 47-59. See also Samuel Sandmel, "The Haggadah Within Scripture," *JBL* 80 (1961) 105-22; *The Hebrew Scriptures* (New York: Knopf, 1963) 340-370.

All of the texts used by both Bloch and Childs are exilic or post-exilic, and the suggestion is that midrash began as soon as the Torah took shape and was "canonized" as Scripture. Bloch states:[18]

> La fixation de l'Ecriture est de la plus grande importance pour la genèse de genre midrashique. Désormais il y a un texte "canonique" sur lequel on va réfléchir, avec lequel on va prier, qui va être objet d'étude, de transmission, d'enseignment, de prédication.

I would like to pursue the origins of midrashic activity and especially its relation to canonization a step further. It is possible that it is actually the other way around: the activity of searching the word of God, in whatever forms it existed in sixth century Israel, was of the greatest importance for the canonization of Scripture. One of the major aims of this study of the barren matriarch traditions is to provide a test case for this hypothesis. Bloch says that,

> On réfléchit sur le passé avec un coeur brisé et on achève le récit grandiose des bienfaits de Dieu d'une part, et de l'infidélite continuelle de son peuple d'autre part.[19]

But what is this reflection of the past, this relating of the recent catastrophe to the ancient Torah story, but midrashic reflection? The two elements are present: the word of God, in the form of the story of the covenant and subsequent sinning of Israel, as told by the prophets, and the adaptation to the present, as the disaster of 587 is interpreted in terms of this story. That the story of Israel's origins and checkered career as God's people was authoritative can be seen in the way virtually all of the prophets cite it as the basis of their prophetic messages.[20]

The tendency to probe the ancient story in the belief that it would yield new meanings existed from before the time of the Exile.[21] Midrash

---

[18]"Midrash," col. 1268.

[19]Ibid.

[20]Jer 2, Isa 51:9-11, etc. See the useful article by Norman Habel on "Appeal to Ancient Tradition as a Literary Form" in the *SBLASP 1972*, 1.34-54.

[21]This is clear already in Gerhard von Rad's classic study, "The Form-critical Problem of the Hexateuch," first published in 1938, now in *The Problem of the Hexateuch and Other Essays* (New York: McGraw-Hill, 1966) 1-78.

Introduction 9

developed naturally as the prophets reflected on the ancient story of Israel's origins in light of the situation in their own time. It developed further when they reflected, in time of crisis, on that same ancient story in their despair in exile. The very same story is given quite different interpretations according to the *Sitz im Leben* in which it is told. How different the story of the Exodus sounds when Micah tells it in the covenant lawsuit in chap 6 or Jeremiah in chap 2, from the way it sounds in the oracle of salvation in Isa 52:3-6, 11-12! In both cases reflection on the Exodus story leads to a word to the people in the present, but it is the prophetic context which determines the interpretation of the story more than anything else.[22] This kind of interpretation of Israelite traditions in the prophetic literature can be called at least proto-midrash.

Now these ancient traditions about Israel's origins were clearly reflected upon before they were crystalized into a written text. In *Torah and Canon*, J. A. Sanders[23] proposes the thesis that the traditions which were preserved and finally canonized were the ones which were able to speak to the exiles in their despair and confusion. It was in the crucible of the exile that the traditions were tested: those which could give life were remembered, and those which could not were forgotten. Sanders refers not only to those traditions which were included in the final shape of the Torah, but also to those which were excluded, notably the conquest of the promised land. But this kind of sifting process could take place only through meditation on the traditions in light of the present circumstance. The traditions were searched in order to find the word of the Lord for that day. It was this process of "searching" the word of God (whether it be written, uttered by a prophet, or sung by a poet) with which Israel was already familiar from the prophetic traditions, which was the impetus of the process of canonization.

Midrash, then, is a thread which runs through the warp and woof of the history of the people of God. Its forms are altered in different ages, and it takes on characteristics from its milieu, but always its aim is constant: to interpret the word of God for the people of God. When Jesus says in John 5:39 "You search the Scriptures because you think that in them you have eternal life," he reflects accurately the Jewish conception of searching the Scriptures.

Comparative midrash is not a new discipline, but rather a new focus on

---

[22] See J. A. Sanders, "Hermeneutics in True and False Prophecy."
[23] And in more detail in "Adaptable for Life."

the literature of the first century Jewish groups. It is a focus which is made possible by the work of many scholars, working in different aspects of first century Judaism. The discovery of the Dead Sea scrolls, new light on the Samaritans, a corrective to the traditional view of the Pharisees, new understanding of the open state of the canon in the first century and the processes by which it became fixed, all have contributed to the demise of the concept of "normative Judaism." Judaism in the first century is now known to be diverse, complex, and rich with striking differences. As a result, the old interest in showing Jesus to be more original or more faithful to the Scriptures than the other Jews of his time has given way to an interest in viewing primitive Christianity as one of many Jewish groups of the first century (and, in fact, to viewing primitive Christianity itself as a complex phenomenon, composed of many groups). The interest now is in the unique self-understanding and way of life of each of these groups as it is revealed in their interpretation of the Scriptures and their interpretation of the events of their own time. As a result there is also a new focus on the function of traditions, especially as seen in the resignification of old traditions in new contexts.

Comparative midrash asks how a given tradition was adapted in different communities which all shared the conviction that the Scriptures would teach them how to live as the people of God in their own times. There are two areas of investigation: the first has to do with form, the second with function.

First, what exegetical rules and hermeneutical principles have the adapters used in order to accomplish their end? Did they appeal to other passages of Scripture to interpret their passage? Did they allude to non-scriptural traditions? Did they interpret certain words of the passage, or deal with the whole context? With whom in the passage did they identify (this is particularly important in identifying the hermeneutics of the ancient exegete, especially if his congregation appears to have identified with a different party)? What literary genres were employed, and how did these genres affect the shape of the resignified tradition? The tools of form criticism and tradition history are basic to our attempt to answer these questions.

Secondly, what question did the midrash attempt to answer? What situation in the community called for a new interpretation of the ancient tradition?

It is in new events and new experiences, usually presupposed and therefore not stated in the midrash, that we must seek the function of the midrash in the community to which it was addressed. What was the question which the community was asking, to which the midrash was providing

Introduction

an answer? Or what circumstance in the community demanded the challenge of a prophetic word or a reminder of their common calling? One of the primary tasks of comparative midrash is to discover what the questions were to which a given adaptation of tradition was providing an answer, and to uncover the presuppositions and common assumptions which the author of the midrash presumed in his community. The approach which is most helpful to date is that of audience criticism. This way has been most fruitfully pursued by J. A. Sanders, especially in three articles dealing with Luke 4, Luke 14, and Phil 2:1-11.[24] Sanders writes:

> One of the extremely valuable emphases in the relatively new field of comparative midrash is that of seeing the contemporization of an ancient tradition in the light of the need of the community which recalled, and reflected upon, the tradition.[25]

Audience criticism presupposes two foci which must engage the exegete: the first is the text itself, and the second is the situation to which the text was first addressed, or as Sanders says, "into which the textual material was first interjected."[26] It is this second focus which is the basis of audience criticism, for it tries to reconstruct the presuppositions of the writer or speaker in addressing the community. These would include, for example, concerns of the community, recent events which might be on the minds of the people, problems which were disturbing the community, and to some extent, values which were presupposed by the community. The important question is how a text was understood by a community. Did they hear it as comforting, challenging, or instructing? The key to this question is the hermeneutics of the writer or speaker. Is he using a Scriptural text, for example, prophetically, to challenge the self-understanding of the community, or constitutively, to endorse the self-understanding of the community?[27]

---

[24]"From Isaiah 61 to Luke 4," *Christianity, Judaism and Other Greco-Roman Cults* (ed. J. Neusner; Leiden: Brill, 1975) 75-106; "The Ethic of Election in Luke's Great Banquet Parable," *Essays in Old Testament Ethics* (ed. Crenshaw and Willis; New York: Ktav, 1974) 247-271; "Dissenting Deities and Philippians 2:1-11," *JBL* 88 (1969) 279-290.
[25]"The Ethic of Election," 248.
[26]Ibid., 248.
[27]"From Isaiah 61 to Luke 4," 97-98. See also "The Dead Sea Scrolls—A Quarter Century of Study," *BA* 36 (December 1973) especially 145-148, and "Hermeneutics," *IDBSup* (Nashville: Abingdon, 1976) 402-407.

One of the main differences between comparative midrash and tradition criticism is evident here.[28] While the task of tradition criticism is to trace the roots and development of a tradition, the main focus of comparative midrash is on the ways in which the tradition was used in the life of various religious communities. One might say that while tradition criticism is interested primarily in the *development* of traditions, comparative midrash is interested primarily in the *function* of traditions. Of course, comparative midrash takes some of its methods from the discipline of tradition criticism; this will be especially clear in the early chapters of our work. However, we hope that the present study will demonstrate that comparative midrash addresses questions which are quite distinct from the questions of tradition criticism.

---

[28]For the most recent work on tradition criticism see Douglas A. Knight, *Rediscovering the Traditions of Israel* (Missoula: Scholars, 1975), and the collection of essays edited by Knight, *Tradition and Theology in the Old Testament* (Philadelphia: Fortress, 1977), and the study by Walter Breugemann, "Next Steps in Tradition Criticism," *Int* 32 (1978) 89-92.

1
The Matriarchs in Genesis

THE SOCIAL CONTEXT

In ancient Israel, as well as in other parts of the ANE, the primary obligation of a married woman was to bear children for her husband, particularly male children. Both the legal and the epic literature of the ANE indicate how pervasive the desire for offspring was among the Israelites and their neighbors.

Of the three Ugaritic epics extant, the Legend of Krt and the Legend of Aqht are concerned with the problem of obtaining heirs. In the first, Krt is left a widower and childless by the catastrophic deaths of his wife and children.[1] In the second, Dnil gives oblations to the gods and lies on a couch of sackcloth because he has no son.[2] In both stories, Baal intercedes for the men before El, and provides a wife "who will bear seven sons" for Krt and life-breath with which the invigorated Dnil will impregnate his wife.

In the Akkadian legend of Etana we read that the childless Etana ascended to heaven on the back of an eagle to obtain the plant of birth and thereby have a son.[3]

Many of the legal documents of the ANE include laws which provide for offspring for the husband of a woman who does not bear him children. There are two categories of such women: priestesses, who cannot bear children by law, and women who are barren. The first case is reflected in

---

[1] Krt lines 1-30, in C. H. Gordon, *Ugaritic Textbook: Texts* (Rome: Pontifical Biblical Institute, 1965) 25. Translation from James B. Pritchard, *Ancient Near Eastern Texts* (Princeton: Princeton University, 1969) 143. (Hereafter cited as *ANET*)

[2] Aqht:I, lines 1-17, in *ANET*, 149-150.

[3] *ANET*, 114-118.

the Code of Hammurabi, numbers 144-147, which provide for the man to marry a lay priestess, or for the hierodule to give him a female slave to provide him with children.[4] The second case occurs in the Nuzi tablets, which include a marriage contract stating that if the wife is unable to bear children she will provide her husband with a woman who will bear him sons, and further, that she may not send the sons away.[5] An Egyptian text from about 1100 B.C.E. indicates that the solution of the female slave bearing children to the husband (whom in this case the wife may adopt) was practiced in Egypt as well as in Mesopotamia.[6]

The Levirate law in Israel is another legal device for providing offspring to a childless person, in this case a widow. The story of Tamar in Genesis 38 tells poignantly of the desire of the childless widow to provide a son for herself and for her dead husband's name. G. W. Coats has recently argued that the right of the widow was not to marry but to conceive a child by her husband's brother.[7]

The concern for children is seen also in the numerous blessings and curses in ANE literature. The wedding of Krt and his bride Hrria is highlighted by a marriage blessing given by El:

> The woman thou tak'st, O Krt,
> The maid thou bring'st into thy court,
> Shall bear seven sons unto thee;
> Yea, eight she'll produce for thee.[8]

The similarities between this blessing and the blessing given to Ruth in Ruth 4:11-12 have been noted in a recent article by Simon Parker.[9] The blessing given to Rebecca as she leaves her father's house to become Isaac's wife is similar:

---

[4] *ANET*, 172.

[5] See E. A. Speiser, *Genesis* (New York: Doubleday, 1964) 120, for a discussion of the text and references to the original.

[6] John van Seters, "The Problem of Childlessness in ANE Law and the Patriarchs of Israel," *JBL* 87 (1968) 401-8.

[7] G. W. Coats, "Widow's Rights: A Crux in the Structure of Gen. 38," *CBQ* 34 (1972) 461-66.

[8] *ANET*, 146.

[9] Simon B. Parker, "The Marriage Blessing in Israelite and Ugaritic Literature," *JBL* 95 (1976) 23-30.

Our sister, be the mother of thousands of ten thousands; and may your descendants possess the gate of those who hate them! Gen 24:60

In the Pentateuch the blessings of fruitfulness given at creation (Gen 1:28), to Noah (Gen 9:7), to Abraham (Gen 12:2-3, 15:5, 17:4-8), Isaac (Gen 26:3-5) and Jacob (Gen 28:13-15) are renewed in the covenant blessings of Deut 28:1-4, contingent upon Israel's obedience. The Covenant Code concludes with the promise that none will be barren in Israel (Exod 23:26 and also in Deut 7:14); the ancient Semitic treaty blessing underlies this promise. Again, in the Holiness Code in Leviticus 26 the blessing of fruitfulness is promised (see esp. v 9).

If an important form of blessing in the ANE is the blessing of fruitfulness, one of the major forms of curse is the curse of barrenness. The curses listed at the end of the Vassal treaties of Esarhaddon include the following:

> May he [Ashur, king of the gods] never grant you fatherhood and attainment of old age.

> May the Lady of the gods, the mistress of creation, cut off birth from your land; may she make rare the cries of little children in the streets and squares.[10]

The Hittite treaty between Suppilulimmas and Kurtiwaza includes among its curses:

> Just as one does not obtain a plant from bubuwahi, even so may you Kurtiwaza with a second wife that you may take, and the Hurri men with your wives, your sons and country have no seed.[11]

Childlessness in the ANE was clearly a serious problem for which as many legal and cultural correctives as possible were devised. Most of these legal and cultural options—polygamy, adoption, and the fathering of a child through the wife's personal slave—occur in the biblical narratives.

---

[10] D. J. Wiseman, *The Vassal-Treaties of Esarhaddon* (British School of Archaeology in Iraq, 1958). See especially Col. VI, lines 415-416 and lines 437-439.

[11] *ANET*, 206.

But there are several striking differences between the biblical materials and the other ANE literature. First, there is virtually no legal material in the Hebrew Bible which provides means for a barren couple to obtain heirs. The sole law dealing with childlessness is the Levirate law in Deut 25:5-10, which does not deal with barrenness. In view of the number of adoption laws in the ANE literature this is surprising. While in the literature of Israel's neighbors childlessness occurs in the legal and narrative literature, in the literature of Israel it occurs only in the narrative literature.

Secondly, in every case except one (Gen 25:21) it is the childless woman who takes action to obtain sons, while in the Ugaritic and Akkadian narratives it is the man who takes action. The biblical stories focus on barren women rather than on childless men.

Finally, the biblical narratives appear to be part of a process of redaction and constant re-interpretation, so that in many cases the meaning of the stories has been shifted from the independent narrative to the context in which it has been set. The stories are not static, but acquire new significance at different stages in Israel's history. It is this characteristic of the Israelite literature with which our investigation will be most concerned, for the meanings of the narratives at various stages of redaction give the best clue to the developing interpretation of barrenness in ancient Israel.

What then do the biblical narratives tell about the meaning of barrenness in Israel? Given the importance of bearing children in the ANE, we would expect that barrenness would be regarded as at least a great misfortune, and more likely as a sign of divine disfavor. This is a common view among scholars who mention barrenness in the Hebrew Bible.[12]

However, a closer examination of the evidence reveals two distinct views of barrenness within the biblical literature. The first, in which barrenness is mentioned as punishment for sin, is found in scattered legal and poetic texts (Lev 20:20-21; 2 Sam 6:23—a somewhat unclear case— Job 18:19; Hos 9:10-18; Prov 30:15-16; Isa 14:22). This view is not presented strongly, nor is it a theme which is very common in the biblical literature, especially in light of its frequency in other ANE literatures. Further, the passages in which it appears are largely from the period of the eighth century to the Exile. Such a collection of passages cannot represent "the biblical view of barrenness," though it does represent one interpretation.

---

[12]E.g. Pedersen, *Israel*, I-II, 71; Kohler, *Hebrew Man*, 42-43; *Oxford Annotated Bible*, 18, 1241.

A more complex view of barrenness occurs in the narrative materials from Genesis through Kings. The passages included are:

Gen 11:30; 15:1-3; 16:17-18; 18:1-15; 21:1-6 (Sarah)
Gen 25:21 (Rebecca)
Gen 29:31-30:24 (Leah and Rachel)
Judges 13 (the wife of Manoah)
1 Samuel 1-2 (Hannah)
2 Kgs 4:8-17 (the Shunammite woman)

These passages share certain elements in common:
1. As opposed to the passages above which represent barrenness as threat of punishment, these narratives offer no reason for the barrenness (other than the indication that it was Yahweh who had closed the womb, for unknown reasons). The narratives do not suggest any fault in the man or the woman which would give an explanation for the problem of barrenness.
2. Unlike the poetic passages cited above, the narratives all deal with individual woman and their stories. The women are not simply symbols or vehicles, but are real people with names and specific situations.
3. In each passage, except 2 Kings 4, the woman conceives because Yahweh hears or sees or remembers the woman.
4. In each passage, except 2 Kings 4, the woman gives birth to a child who becomes a significant figure in the biblical history. (The deviation of 2 Kings 4 from the categories 3 and 4 make it an important witness to the problem of the literary form of the narratives.)

However, these narratives represent a variety of literary forms and sources, as well as contexts, and they are not by any means all of a kind. There is a tendency among scholars who mention the motif of barrenness in passing to lump all of these narratives together as witnesses to one motif. Since Gunkel labeled this theme a "favorite saga motif" ("Lange Unfruchtbarkeit der Mutter vor den Geburt des Kindes ist ein beliebtes Sagenmotif"),[13] it has been commonly assumed that this is the source of the motif, and that the stories are of the birth of a hero/divine child type outlined by Otto Rank in his now classic study, *The Myth of the Birth of the Hero*. But this assumption is not demonstrated either by Gunkel or those who follow him, and important distinctions between the narratives

---

[13]Hermann Gunkel, *Genesis* (Göttingen, 1922) 294.

are overlooked. In fact, the narratives have never been seriously studied as a corpus, and many questions still remain unanswered.

Why was the motif of the barren woman who finally gave birth to a son so cherished in Israel's sacred traditions? To what issue in the eleventh-tenth centuries did it respond? Did it spring up independently in individual narratives, or are some of the narratives related? At what point in the development of the patriarchal traditions did the motif of the barren mothers enter? Is it part of the most ancient tradition or is it a later element? The source and function of these narratives has not yet been understood or explicated—not because of any overwhelming difficulty, but simply because the narratives have not been seriously studied and the questions have not been asked.

THE PATRIARCHAL NARRATIVES

Sarah

When one studies these narratives of the mothers of Israel, it immediately becomes apparent that the Sarah traditions are the most complex. This is because the issue of Abraham's childlessness occurs not once but six times in the Abraham cycle, in a diversity of sources and traditions. Further, the Sarah traditions are different from all of the others in a very important aspect: there are in fact two traditions about Sarah. One tradition is that Sarah was barren; the other is that both Sarah and Abraham were old and childless. While being old and childless might imply barrenness, the two traditions of old age and of barrenness do not occur together within the Abraham cycle.

Of the six passages dealing with Abraham's childlessness, Genesis 18 contains the oldest material. The story of the three visitors to whom Abraham shows hospitality is almost universally attributed to a source prior to the Yahwist. The narrative has undergone redaction from a more primitive form to its present form, with some of the seams still showing. The conflicting references to the visitors as three men (vv 2-9) and as Yahweh (vv 1, 10, 13-14) indicate redaction. The main features of the narrative are those of the "reward for hospitality" narrative which is common in the literature of the ancient world. The narrative has been form-critically analyzed many times, and the basic outlines of the ancient

The Matriarchs in Genesis 19

hospitality legend have been recognized.[14] One or more gods in disguise visit a mortal, who shows them hospitality and is then rewarded by the gods, usually with a son in his old age. What has not been recognized, however, is the condition of Sarah and Abraham. Sarah laughs at the promise of a son not because she is barren but because she is old (אחרי עדנה היתה-לי בלתי) and Abraham is old (זקן ואדני). There is no mention of barrenness.

There are many parallels to this story in ancient mythology; the one commonly referred to is the visit of the three gods Zeus, Poseidon and Hermes to the peasant Hyrieus.[15] In return for his hospitality to the disguised gods, Hyrieus is granted a son in his old age, Orion, who is born ten months later. The aged Baucis and Philomen are similarly visited by gods in disguise and granted a son for their hospitality.[16] In 2 Kings 4 the Shunammite woman and her husband, old and childless, are given a son for their hospitality to the prophet Elisha. In this story the prophet, the man of God, has taken the place of the gods, but the form of the hospitality narrative has remained the same.

Genesis 18 has been edited by the Yahwist, though the ancient tale is left surprisingly intact.[17] The fulfillment of the promise of a son must originally have been a part of the story, as form critically it is part of the hospitality narratives, but it was separated from its original context and made part of the Ishmael-Isaac conflict in Gen 21:1. By separating the climax of the story the Yahwist also continued his theme of the delay of the promise and heightened the tension in the Abraham story.

This legend is not the birth of a hero type, for there is no emphasis on the child; he is not named, nor is his destiny stated. The focus is instead on the parents and their piety and reward. The antiquity of the narrative suggests that it is the original version of the Pentateucal tradition of the childlessness of Abraham and Sarah.

---

[14]Gerhard von Rad, *Genesis* (Philadelphia: Westminster, 1961) 200; Gunkel, *Genesis*, 173-4; Theodore Gaster, *Myth, Legend and Custom in the Old Testament*, 156-7, 518-19; John Skinner, *Genesis* (Edinburgh: Clark, 1910) 302-3.
[15]See especially Gunkel, *Genesis*, 200.
[60]Ovid, *Metamorphoses*, 8.616ff and Gunkel, *Genesis*, 193.
[17]One need not argue for direct borrowing of the motif from these sources; Gaster's work shows that hospitality to the gods which was rewarded by a son was a common motif. 2 Kgs 4:8-17 is evidence that this motif was known in ninth century Israel.

The giving of the promise in Genesis 17 appears to follow the tradition established in Genesis 18. While the Priestly editings are dominant throughout, the skeleton of the ancient narrative is still visible. The laughter of Abraham in response to the promise is difficult to explain except as an influence of Genesis 18. The locution that Sarah will bear a son at this season next year כעת חיה appears to follow Gen 18:10. The phrase כעת חיה, occurring only here and in 2 Kgs 4:16, in the Elisha hospitality narrative, is difficult, and the more common למועד הזה of Gen 17:21 may represent an attempt to clarify the already obscure כעת חיה.[18]

Most significantly, the objection to the announcement of Isaac's birth in Genesis 17 is not that Sarah is barren but that both she and Abraham are old. The announcement of the birth of Isaac in Genesis 17 then appears to be based on traditions which first occurred in the hospitality narrative of Genesis 18. It has been suggested, in fact, that Genesis 17 is itself a healing narrative, patterned after Genesis 18.[19] However, the elements of the healing narrative have been so eclipsed by the covenant formulation and the birth announcement that it is impossible to demonstrate this. We suggest only that Genesis 18 is the basis for the tradition of the promise of a son to an aged Sarah and Abraham, and for the response of laughter to the promise.

Where then do we find the tradition that Sarah was barren? It does not occur in the most ancient tradition about the birth of Isaac, so we must look to the next level of tradition. The first mention of Sarah's barrenness comes in a Yahwistic interpolation in vv 28-30 of the genealogy in Genesis 11. These verses establish the situation in Abram's family, a prelude to Genesis 12. The Yahwist tells us in v 28 that Abram has one brother, Nahor (of whom we hear in Genesis 24, as the grandfather of Rebecca), and in v 29 he tells us the names of the wives of Abram and Nahor. In v 30, the additional piece of information that Sarah was barren is striking, for several reasons. First, it breaks the pattern of genealogy; no information other than names, length of life, descendants and deaths are recorded in this genealogy. Since Nahor's sons are not named, there would be nothing strange in not mentioning Abram's, either. But the mention of Sarah's barrenness is an addition which is curious in the context of the genealogy. Further, the locution is very strong; not only does

---

[18] See the discussion in Robert W. Neff, "The Birth and Election of Isaac in the Priestly Tradition," *Biblical Research* 15 (1970) 5-18, and O. Loretz, "Kᶜt ḥyh —'wie jetztums Jahr' Gen 18:10," *Bib* 43 (1962) 75-78.

[19] Neff, "The Birth and Election of Isaac."

the text say עקרה, barren, but also that she had no child, a phrase which is redundant with עקרה. The Yahwist is here clearly signaling what will be for him an important theme.

The purpose of Gen 11:30 in the Yahwist's plan is clear; it establishes the impossible situation into which Yahweh's promise of numerous descendants is given. As the promise occurs already in Genesis 12, just a few verses later, the tension surrounding the promise is felt immediately. But the significance of the Yahwist's addition should not be limited to the function of Gen 11:30 in light of Genesis 12. By his elaboration of the tradition of the aged couple's childlessness, he has introduced a new element into the Abraham cycle. While the original tradition of Abraham's childlessness arises only in the context of the divine reward, and provides a situation for which the gods can bestow their gracious gifts, in the Yahwistic context Abraham's childlessness becomes a serious problem which appears precisely to prevent the fulfillment of the deity's gracious promise. By placing the statements of Sarah's barrenness in the genealogy of Chapter 11, the Yahwist has shown his intent to make her childlessness a problem from the very beginning.

> Saras Kinderlösigkeit ist die Voraussetzung für fast alle folgenden Erzahlungen, auch für den Auszug: der Glaube Abrahams an Gottes Verheissung, er solle einst ein grosses Volk werden 12:2, ist um so bewunderungswirdiger als er damals noch night einmal einen einzigen Sohn hatte.[20]

Genesis 16 is an important part of the tradition of Sarah's barrenness, for the conception of Ishmael by Hagar and Abraham is presented as Sarah's solution to her barrenness. But what was the original function of the narrative, and what is its function in its present context?

There is general agreement about certain aspects of Genesis 16 and its relation to Genesis 21 which should be stated here.[21] First, the narrative in Genesis 16 is older in form than the narrative in Genesis 21. However, while the form of Genesis 16 is older, certain elements of Genesis 21 appear to be the more original. For example, the relationship between Isaac and Ishmael is basically one of strife (Gen 16:12, Gen 25:18, Ps

---

[20] Gunkel, *Genesis*, 162.
[21] See Gunkel, Skinner, von Rad and Neff. See especially Rudolf Kilian's *Die Vorpriesterlichen Abrahamsüberlieferungen* (Bonn: Peter Hanstein, 1966) 88-95, on Sarah's barrenness as a secondary addition to explain the flight of Hagar and the birth of Ishmael in the wilderness.

83:7). Genesis 16, while it preserves the ancient oracle, portrays strife between the two women rather than between the two sons.

Secondly, the narrative of Genesis 16 is almost universally attributed to the Yahwist. Finally, the original purpose of the narrative in Genesis 16 appears to be the etiology of the name of the well Beer-lahai-roi and its designation as a cultic place. Martin Noth has dealt incisively with Genesis 16 and 21 in his work on the Ishmael and Isaac traditions:

> In terms of its content as a story of birth, the J version of Gen. 16 is not only more original in form in comparison to the E version in Gen. 21:8-12, but has also retained an original element in the connection with the groundwater well of Beer-lahai-roi. Now traditio-historically Ishmael was primarily the brother of Isaac, and only secondarily did he become, along with Isaac, the son of Abraham. Indeed, Isaac and Ishmael were "brothers" by virtue of being ancestors of two clan groups who shared in common the water of the well Beer-lahai-roi and who participated in the cult of the local deity worshipped there, El-Roi.[22]

The etiological interest in the name of Ishmael testifies to the original significance of the narrative about the origins of the eponymous ancestor of the Ishmaelites. Noth concludes that this is in fact the most ancient function of the narrative.

> The ultimate basis of the transmitted narrative is a presumably Ishmaelite tradition according to which Ishmael, the ancestor of nomads, was born in the wilderness at a place where a deity showed his mother the well Beer-lahai-Roi (this original element of the tradition is preserved in Gen 21:19 E); and at the same time, the deity, by apppearing there, established the present sanctity of the place.[23]

What then is the origin of the story of Sarah's use of Hagar to obtain a son for herself and Abraham, because "Yahweh has prevented me from bearing children"? Sarah's solution is often referred to as one which is common in the Tanak and in the ancient world. However, it occurs only twice in the Tanak: here and in Gen 30:1-24, so it can hardly be called a

---

[22] *History of the Pentateuchal Traditions* (Englewood Cliffs, NJ: Prentice Hall, 1972) 108.
[23] Ibid., 108, n. 312.

common biblical motif. To understand how the theme of Sarah's barrenness functions in Genesis 16 we must discern the stage at which it entered the tradition of Ishmael's birth. All of the references to Sarah's barrenness thus far have proved to be from the Yahwist, and have functioned as part of his theme of obstacles to the promise and the delay of its fulfillment. Whether Genesis 16 also follows this pattern cannot be decided until it is studied together with Gen 30:1-24, the other occurrence of the barren wife giving her slave to her husband.

Rachel and Leah

Gen 29:31-30:24 is the account of the birth of the twelve sons of Jacob. It is generally agreed that this narrative represents a reading back into the patriarchal age traditions which were not developed and formalized until the early monarchy.[24] The system of the twelve tribes is a schematic view of early Israel. Relating the twelve to one common father is a further development in the history of the tradition which helped unify Israel and give her a past which related to her present.[25]

But while it is agreed that this narrative is a "late" and highly schematized formulation, there is no agreement on the pre-history of the tradition of the tribes. This is a complex area, which we need not enter into here, as our interest is in the redaction of the twelve tribe tradition rather than its pre-history. However, in our inquiry concerning Rachel's barrenness it will be helpful to examine some of the theses concerning the origins of the Rachel and Leah traditions and their relation to the Jacob cycle.

In a study of the origins of the traditions about the tribes, Sigmund Mowinckel has provided a valuable tradition history of Gen 29:31-30:24. Citing the rules of folklore, Mowinckel assumes that Jacob and Israel were originally two distinct persons.

> Nun ist es ein folkloristisches und traditionsgeschichtliches "Gesetz," dass, wenn eine Person unter zwei ganz verschie-

---

[24]See, for example, Noth, *Pentateuchal Traditions*, 99-100; von Rad, *Genesis*, 291; Speiser, *Genesis*, 232.

[25]See John Bright, *A History of Israel* (Philadelphia: Westminster, 1972) 156-158; Noth, *The History of Israel* (New York: Harper and Row, 1960) 85-97; *Pentateuchal Traditions*, 100.

denen Namen auftritt, dass auf einer Zusammenschmelzung zweier ursprünglich selbstandiger Personen beruht.[26]

Israel was the *heros eponymos* of a group which moved from the Sinai peninsula into Canaan, and united with some of the *Habiru* already settled in Canaan. These two distinct groups united under the name of Israel, the tradition of the Exodus, and the God Yahweh. However, no traditions about the "original" Israel remain; all of the material we have about Israel is from the Jacob history.

The tradition of Jacob is more complex. He was linked with specific locales in central Palestine and in the East Jordan region. The tradition also indicates an association with the area of Northwest Mesopotamia, through the cultural context and personal names in the Jacob narratives. The groups from Northwest Mesopotamia and the groups from Sinai, then, both migrating into Palestine, became associated with each other, and the resulting group took the traditions of Jacob and the name of Israel.[27]

If Israel and Jacob were originally two separate groups, to which group did Rachel and Leah belong? Mowinckel answers that Rachel and Leah are an integral part of the Jacob-Laban saga, and that the Northwest Semitic customs reflected in the Jacob narratives about the women indicate that they are a constitutive part of the Jacob tradition.

Mowinckel argues that Rachel—Bilah and Leah—Zilpah were both originally two aspects of fertility goddesses in Northwest Mesopotamia. However, his evidence is not convincing (e.g., the reference to Rachel weeping for her children in Jer 31:15 indicates that she was considered to be alive in her tomb!). If this were the case, it would hardly be possible to reconstruct such a tradition from the meagre evidence we have. I think rather that Noth's suggestion that the two women entered the traditions through their association with the East Jordan Jacob is more sensible.[28] In any case, the older view that Rachel and Leah were personifications of the tribal groups cannot be demonstrated. Unlike Jacob, Rachel and Leah do not appear to have entered Israelite tradition as fully drawn characters; they are fleshed out by the Israelite redactors of the earlier traditions.

The union of the separate groups and the common adaptation of their

---

[26]"'Rahelstamme' und 'Leastamme'," *Von Ugarit nach Qumran* (eds. J. Hemple and L. Rost; Berlin: Töpelmann, 1955) 131.
[27] See Noth, *Pentateuchal Traditions*, 54-58.
[28] *Pentateuchal Traditions*, 150.

traditions probably occurred at some point during the settlement of Canaan; however, the schematic formalization into a twelve-tribe system may not have been so early. The significance of the number twelve for tribal groups is attested by the OT traditions themselves; e.g., the list of twelve Aramean tribes in Gen 22:20-24, the twelve Ishmaelite tribes in Gen 25:13-16, and the twelve Edomite tribes in 36:10-14. The tradition of the twelve sons of Jacob probably represents a schematic ideal view of the origins of Israel rather than a historically accurate one. What then is the basis for the distribution of the twelve sons among the four women? Mowinckel suggests geographical and political reasons:

> Das dawidische Zwölf-Stämme-Schema stellt somit eine Mischung von Tradition, geographischer Lage und politischer Theorie dar. Die Verteilung auf die beiden Hauptfrauen Lea und Rahel hat den Grund, dass nach der Lage der Dinge: Geographie, Geschichte und Kult-tradition nur Josef und Benjamin der Rahel zugeteilt werden konnten. Aus geschichtlichen (und usprünglich auch geographischen) Gründen konnte aber Dan nicht ganz von der Joseftradition losgerissen werden; das hat ihn zum Sohn der Rahel-Magd Bilha gemacht, und die geographische Lage hat ihm Naftali zum Vollbruder gegeben. Alle die anderen mussten Leasöhne werden bzw. bleiben.[29]

But what is the purpose of this curious narrative? Noth calls the passage "very artificial in structure";[30] in such a passage, however, the question of function becomes all the more pressing. Why was such a narrative constructed? While it links the twelve sons to a common father, it does not explain the nature of the tribes, for the focus is not on the sons but on the mothers. Clearly the narrative intended to trace the twelve tribes back to a common ancestor, to give Israel a strong identity which was firmly rooted in the patriarchal age. This was one function of much of the editing of old traditions which occurred in the period of the monarchy. However, the focus of the story on the triangle of Rachel-Jacob-Leah indicates another theme which was important to the editor. The etymologies of the names makes this clear; the two sisters, not their sons, are the center of the story. In contrast, Genesis 49 draws the characters of the tribal ancestors in detail and relates them to the future of

---

[29] Mowinckel, "'Rahelstamme' und 'Leastamme'," 150.
[30] Ibid., 100.

each tribe. Gen 29:31-30:24 on the other hand is not simply a narrative about the origins of the tribal ancestors; it is rather a very tense drama about the two wives of Jacob. The narrative as it now stands is the work of the Yahwist, though of course it contains much older material which the Yahwist has worked into a highly structured narrative. Noth calls the narrative artificial in structure while Jacob, in his commentary on Genesis, refers to it as symmetrical.

> Die Anordnung is nicht chronologisch, sondern sachlich: 4 Kinder der Lea—2 der Magd Rahels—2 der Magd Leas—abermals 2 der Lea—der Sohn Rahels = a-b-b-a-b.[31]

Unifying this structure is the theme of the competition between the two women for sons and for love of the husband.

> Eine dramatische Gliederung erhält diese lange Reihe: 1. durch den Ausbruch der Verzweiflung bei Rahel (30:1 ff); 2. durch den Zwischenfall mit den dudaim. Im ubrigen ist der Aufbau gleichmässig, etwaige Abweichungen sind entweder sachlich begründet oder gehören zu den unerheblichen Varianten, die mit jeder Wiederholung verbunden sind.[32]

This theme of the struggle between the two women pervades the entire narrative, even to the extent of influencing the etymologies of the names of the sons. Of the eleven sons whose births are described in this narrative, the names of eight are related directly to the antagonism between Rachel and Leah. The Hebrew names have either a literal meaning, are tribal designations or have meanings which are no longer known. But the interpretations given in Gen 29:31-30:24 do not follow these meanings; instead they are governed by the context of the narrative, and they sharpen the motif of competition between the two women.

Following is a list of the names with their literal meanings and the meanings attributed to them in Gen 29:31-30:24.[33]

In almost every case the original meaning of the name has been expanded and re-interpreted; with the birth of each son the struggle between the sisters is continued and the tension of the narrative is

---

[31]B. Jacob, *Genesis* (Berlin: Schocken, 1934) 601.
[32]Ibid., 593.
[33]For the older meanings see M. Noth, *Die Israeliten Personennamen* (Stuttgart: Kohlhammer, 1928), and the *IDBSup* 619-621.

heightened. Several of the etymologies are particularly interesting because the older etymology has been preserved alongside the special etymology which was devised for the narrative, e.g., Zebulun and Joseph.[34]

Name	Literal Meaning	Interpreted Meaning In Gen 29:31-30:24
Reuben	behold a son	because Yahweh has looked on my affliction, surely now my husband will love me
Simeon	God has heard	because Yahweh has heard that I am hated he has given me this son also (a play on שנא שמע)
Levi	uncertain	now this time my husband will be joined to me because I have borne him three sons
Judah	uncertain	this time I will praise Yah
Dan	he has judged	God has judged me, and has also heard my voice and given me a son
Naphtali	uncertain	with mighty wrestlings have I wrestled with my sister and have prevailed
Gad	fortune	good fortune
Asher	happy	happy am I
Issacher	uncertain	You must come in to me, for I have hired you with my son's mandrakes. God has given me hire, because I gave my maid to my husband

---

[34] See the very interesting study by David Daube on the technical meaning of "hire," "Law in the Hebrew Narratives," in *Studies in Biblical Law* (Cambridge: University Press, 1947) 1-73, especially 16-29 on שכר.

Zebulun	exaltation, dowry	God has endowed me with a good dowry; now my husband will honor me, because I have borne him six sons
Joseph	he causes to be added	God has taken away my reproach. May Yahweh add to me another son.

A comparison of the motifs and the linguistic peculiarities of Gen 29:31-30:24 with Gen 16:1-6 reveals a striking similarity. The central characters in both narratives are two women and one man, all members of the same household. One woman, the more beloved, is barren; the other, who has an inferior status, is fertile. The secondary woman sees her pregnancy as a triumph over her more loved companion. The barren woman becomes desperate and devises a scheme to deal with the situation. Sarah drives Hagar out and Rachel bargains with Leah to get her mandrakes. Further, both Sarah and Rachel give their personal maids to their husbands to obtain a legal son. This practice is not mentioned anywhere else in the Tanak but in Genesis 16 and 30. In both stories, the schemes of the women fail to bring the desired results, and the solution comes only when Yahweh intervenes and opens their wombs. It is interesting that neither woman ever called on Yahweh to open her womb; the long desired pregnancy occurred because of divine plans rather than because of human maneuvering.

Finally, there is a similarity between the sons who are granted to the barren women: in both cases the one son born to the beloved wife is the best loved son and is the most significant in the story of Israel's origins. Isaac receives the divine promise, and Joseph becomes a large and prosperous tribe.

The striking similarity between the motifs of the two narratives is further underlined by numerous verbal parallels. Not only are the circumstances of Sarah and Rachel similar, but the terms used to describe their actions are almost identical:

Like Sarah, Rachel did not at first bear children for her husband:

Gen 30:1	לא ילדה ליעקב
Gen 16:1	לא ילדה לו

As Sarah sent Abraham in to Hagar to obtain a son, so Rachel sent Jacob in to her maid Bilhah:

Gen 30:3   בא אליה ותלד על ברכי
Gen 16:2   בא-נא אל-שפחתי

Both women use the phrase אבנה ממנה

Gen 30:3   ואבנה גם-אנכי ממנה
Gen 16:2   אולי אבנה ממנה

In both stories the phrase ותתן . . . לאשה confirms the legal nature of the transaction and emphasizes that the plan is initiated by the women:

Gen 30:4   ותתן-לו את-בלהה שפחתה לאשה
Gen 16:3   ותתן אתה לאברם אישה לו לאשה

The phrase ליבא אל- follows the phrase ותתן . . . לאשה in both narratives:

Gen 30:4   ויבא אליה יעקב
Gen 16:4   ויבא אל-הגר

The desired results follow:

Gen 30:5   ותהר בלהה ותלד ליעקב בן
Gen 16:4   ותהר

    The similarity in motif and the correspondence of phrases in Gen 16:1-6 and Gen 30:1-4 indicate a common author. As both narratives are almost unanimously attributed to the Yahwist, these similarities are not so surprising. What is significant is that in both cases the barrenness of the central female figure and the devices she employs to circumvent her problem can be traced to the Yahwist. We have seen above how Sarah's barrenness was a motif created by the Yahwist (using the narrative preserved in Genesis 18 as a foundation). In a similar way the tradition of the twelve eponymous heroes and their common ancestor was the basis for the Yahwist's story in Gen 29:31-30:24, and the birth of Ishmael tradition was the basis for his story in Genesis 16. The emphasis on the matriarchs' barrenness and the tension between the two wives is probably not part of the original tradition, but is a theological theme which is woven into the Yahwist's history of the patriarchs.

Rebecca

The mention of Rebecca's barrenness is the least complex of the materials dealing with the matriarchs, and we will deal with it summarily here. That Rebecca was barren is mentioned in only one verse in Genesis, a verse which is almost certainly from the Yahwist. It occurs in the midst of what appears to be an ancient tradition about the origins of the struggle between Jacob and Esau, including an oracle from an unknown source. The narrative in Gen 25:19-26 does not depend on Rebecca's barrenness; the story would proceed exactly the same whether v 21 were omitted or not. The only possible argument for its basis in another tradition is found in vv 20 and 26. If both of these verses are from the Priestly editors, or from their source, v 21 could have been inserted to explain why Jacob waited twenty years between marriage and parenthood.[35] However, v 21 reflects Yahwistic language. עתר is unique to the Yahwist in the Hexateuch, as is עקרה.[36] Either the verse is from the Yahwist, inserted to continue his pattern of the wives of the patriarchs being barren; or it was inserted later, in a conscious imitation of the Yahwist's style, to explain vv 20 and 26. As the Isaac materials are very sparse and the Yahwist apparently had few traditions with which to work (e.g., other wives, other sons), Rebecca's barrenness could not be elaborated in the same way as Sarah's and Rachel's. That it was important for her to be barren is clear from the way in which v 21 has been inserted, with no real purpose in the narrative, no link to an earlier tradition and no mention again. Isaac simply prays for Rebecca and her womb is opened; there is no attempt by Rebecca to solve her problem, no mention of anguish, and no hint of human conflict over her barrenness. This is probably explained by the lack of any useful traditions in the Isaac cycle with which the Yahwist could work; he therefore simply stated that Rebecca was barren and that Yahweh granted her a son.

I have tried to show that the motif of the barren matriarch is not simply a "*beliebtes Sagenmotif*," but is a literary creation of the Yahwist, who reinterpreted ancient traditions about the birth of sons into a pattern of barrenness and subsequent fertility which he followed for all three of

---

[35]Von Rad points out that the entire section of vv 21-28 does not originate in an ancient saga, but is rather a preface, a loose string of statements which gives facts necessary for the following stories. *Genesis*, 260.

[36]Deut 7:14 is the only occurrence of עקרה outside of the Yahwistic narratives about the matriarchs.

the matriarchs. If the literary analysis is correct, and the narratives about the wives of the patriarchs all come from the same source, the initial question of what this motif means becomes all the more pertinent. Why did the Yahwist add this aspect to the patriarchal narratives? What issue was he addressing by his repetition of the theme of barrenness with the story of each matriarch?

Several excellent studies on the work of the Yahwist have illuminated the function of the Yahwistic history in the time of the United Kingdom, thereby revealing at least some of the Yahwist's purpose. In an important work titled *Jahwist und Priesterschrift*, Marie Louise-Henry discusses "Das Jahwistische Geschichtsbild als Hybris bannendes Regulativ im Zeitalter der Reichsgrundung." Having shown the pessimistic and un-idealized nature of the primeval and the patriarchal histories, she asks:

> Was veranlasste diesem Erzähler, der den Glanz solchen Aufsteigs gesehen hatte, zumindest noch irgendwie im Bereich seiner Ausstrahlung stand, gleichwohl so grundsätzlich negativ über das Wesen des Menschen zu urteilen? Was bewog ihn, der doch, wie die erwähnten Sprüche zu erweisen scheinen, an seine Zeit nicht prinzipiell den Massstab prophetischer Kritik anlegte, dem Menschen seiner Tage eine Sicht der Dinge zu eröffnen, die wie eine Aufforderung wirken musste, die nationale Kraftenfaltung nicht als Erweis eigenen Vermögens oder als Bestätigung eigenen Verdienstes, sondern als vorläufiges Ergebnis einer Kette von Bewahrungen und Begnadungen zu verstehen? Denn eben auf diese Erkenntnis hin war die Ur- und Vätergeschichte angelegt.[37]

By emphasizing the failures of the patriarchs, and by the significance of the covenant ceremony at Sinai (far more important in the Yahwist's work than the conquest tradition), the Yahwist underlined the dependence of Israel on divine grace rather than on her own achievements.

> So ruft der Jahwist seine im Zeichen glückhaften Aufstiegs lebenden Zeitgenossen mit unnachsichtiger Härte zur Sache. Er macht die Orientierung an göttlicher Willensnorm als Voraussetzung realistischer Menschenerkenntnis zum Gebot einer Stunde, in der sich bescheideneren Geistern die Deutung alter Auszugs-, Wander- und Landnahmertraditionen im Sinne

---

[37] *Jahwist und Priesterschrift* (Calwer, 1960) 15.

völkischer Prärogativen nur zu leicht nahelegen konnten. Er bannt die Gefahr möglicher religiöser Hybris, indem er sein Volk ernaut unter den verpflichtenden Anspruch Gottes stellt; denn dieser allein mochte im Geschehen seiner Tage als geeignet erscheinen, eine Überbewertung menschlichen Vermögens und Seins abzuwehren und echtes religiöses Leben zu bewahren.[38]

THE FUNCTION OF THE MOTIF

The motif of the barren matriarchs functions in the Yahwistic saga to demonstrate three points about Israel's identity and about how she should live to fulfill this identity.

1. It is the same Lord who opens and closes the womb, and his name is Yahweh. In tenth century Israel the question of who controlled the forces of fertility was a crucial one. It was difficult for the Israelites to accept that Yahweh, whom they had known as a liberator God, was also the Lord of fertility in the new land of Canaan. The stories of the women whose wombs were opened and closed according to Yahweh's will were part of the monotheizing theology of the Yahwist. Monotheism was by no means generally accepted in tenth century Israel, as the books of Samuel and Kings clearly indicate, and the stories of the barren women functioned to show that the gift of life came from Yahweh alone.

2. If the fulfillment of the promise to the Patriarchs was unfolding in the present, then Israel depended on Yahweh for life in the present just as she had in the past. No descendants came to Abraham, Isaac and Jacob save through the gracious will of Yahweh. The miraculous birth of Isaac does not function as a credential for Isaac's heroic nature, as such stories usually did in the ancient world, but rather as a sign that Isaac's birth was a gift from Yahweh and was part of his unfolding plan for Israel.

3. The stories also functioned as a literary device in the service of the Yahwist's theme of obstacles to the promise. The history of the Patriarchs presented one obstacle after another which, according to human standards, would prevent the fulfillment of the promise. The Yahwist edited much of the ancient saga material so that it would heighten the suspense of how Yahweh would overcome these obstacles to fulfill his promise. The stories of the barren matriarchs functioned not only as an important part of the obstacle theme, but also as a graphic illustration of the integrity of Yahweh in fulfilling his promise.

---

[38]Ibid., 19.

THE YAHWIST'S METHODS

What are the principles of interpretation which underlie the Yahwist's use of the ancient patriarchal material? In adapting pre-Israelite and early Israelite traditions to his history of the promise, the Yahwist employed certain principles through which he gave the ancient material theological coherence.

1. First and most significantly, the Yahwist presupposes monotheism. As we noted above, monotheism was by no means generally accepted by the Israelites of the monarchy; the Yahwist was part of a minority who argued for the oneness of God.

2. The Yahwist presupposed that any dreadful state, no matter how irredeemable in human eyes, could be used by Yahweh in the fulfillment of his promise. Not only could he, but Yahweh seemed to prefer working through those who were least likely and least able to do what he needed. Human categories of who has status and who is despised are skewed by the Yahwist's affirmation of Yahweh's power to turn weakness to strength and death to life. In the Joseph narrative the Yahwist speaks through Joseph when, greeting his frightened brothers, he says, "You meant evil against me; but God meant it for good, to bring it about that many people should be kept alive, as they are today" (Gen 50:20). The idea that Yahweh used that which was feared and despised by men for good occurs throughout the Yahwistic materials, and the stories of the barren matriarchs are primary examples of Yahweh's use of evil for good.

2
Hannah

The infancy narrative of Samuel presents us with a complex interweaving of traditions and literary forms. The narrative includes material about the birth of Samuel, the corruption of Eli's sons in the sanctuary at Shiloh, the prophecy of the end of Eli's priesthood, and the call of Samuel as a prophet. It is, therefore, not simply an infancy narrative, but rather a collection of literary works reflecting diverse traditions which have been skillfully united into a unique form. The narrator has united the diverse traditions by the structural device of a theme: the growth of Samuel in Yahweh's favor and the decline of the house of Eli. The editorial links, which all refer to the growth of Samuel (2:11, 2:18-21, 2:26, 3:1, 3:19), are a constant refrain. These refrains about Samuel's growth alternate with various episodes in the downfall of Eli's sons, forming a contrast of piety and corruption. Whatever the original diversity of traditions in 1 Samuel 1-3, the final form presents a carefully structured and unified narrative.

Studies of the narrative have focused largely on the question of source and form criticism.[1] This may reflect the period in which most of the studies were done, the first part of this century, when source criticism was one of the primary interests of biblical studies. While the questions of original forms and sources is pertinent to 1 Samuel 1-3, these forms have

---

[1] The significant studies are J. Dus, "Die Geburtslegends Samuels 1 Sam. 1," *RSO* 43 (1968) 163-194; I. Hylander, *Die Literarische Samuel-Saul-Komplex* (Uppsala, 1932); R. Press, "Der Prophet Samuel," *ZAW* 36 (1938) 177-225; J. Schäfers, "I Sam. 1-15: Literarkritisch Untersucht," *BZ* 5 (1907) 1-21, and the commentary of H. Stoebe, *Das Erste Buch Samuel* (Gütersloh: Gütersloher Verlagshaus Gerd Mohn, 1973). The only studies which move significantly beyond source criticism are H. Hertzberg, *I and II Samuel* (1964) and J. Bourke, "Samuel and the Ark, A Study in Contrasts," *Dominican Studies* 7 (1954) 73-103.

been edited with such unifying skill that it is almost impossible to demonstrate the precise origin of a given tradition or the exact correlation of one tradition to another. However, a few conclusions seem to be fairly well grounded and can be assumed here as working hypotheses.

1. 1 Samuel 1-3 is composed of the originally independent traditions of Eli at Shiloh and of the birth of Samuel, which have been united into one narrative. The relation between Samuel and Shiloh is not seen outside this narrative.[2]

2. The tradition of the birth of Samuel may be based on a more ancient narrative of the birth of Saul. The etiology of Samuel's name from the root שאל and the frequency of this root in the narrative (1:20, 1:28, 2:20) suggest this. Further, the picture of Saul in 1 Samuel as a charismatic leader in the tradition of the judges indicates that Saul was originally a hero in the judges tradition and may, like Samson, have had a birth narrative.[3]

3. There is a literary relationship between 1 Samuel 1 and Judges 13. The recurrence of phrases from Judges 13 and 1 Samuel 1 indicates interdependence.

Judg 13:2   ויהי איש אחד מצרעה ממשפחת הדני
                 ושמו מנוח
1 Sam 1:1   ויהי איש אחד מן-הרמתים צופים
                 . . . ושמו אלקנה

Both narratives begin in the same classical story form: "There was a certain man from X and his name was Y."

---

[2]Only Press argues that Samuel was originally a prophet attached to Shiloh, in opposition to Eli, as Amos opposed Amaziah at Bethel. However, there is no agreement on the way in which the two traditions came together, or on the motive for combining them.

[3]See especially Hylander and Dus, who attempt to discern how the histories of Saul and Samuel became conflated. The relationship between the traditions about Samson, Saul and Samuel is probably locked into the pre-literary stage of our material; while fascinating, it is highly speculative. The interesting point is that even at a very early stage the traditions about one hero became authoritative enough to serve as a type, or at least as an influence, in order to imbue the life of a newer hero with authority and to give him the proper "credentials." A kind of proto-midrash was practiced on the traditions even at this early stage.

Judg 13:2	ואשתו עקרה ולא ילדה
1 Sam 1:2	ולו שתי נשים . . . ולחנה אין ילדים

Both men had wives who had not borne any children.

Judg 13:24	ויגדל הנער ויברכהו יהוה
1 Sam 2:21	ויגדל הנער שמואל עם-יהוה

Both boys grew up in a special relationship to Yahweh.

Judg 13:4	ואל-תשתי יין ושכר
1 Sam 1:15	ויין ושכר לא שתיתי

Both mothers abstained from wine and strong drink during the pregnancy.

While the relationship between the two narratives is clear, it is difficult to say in which direction the influence goes. The evidence suggests that Samuel's story has been influenced by Samson's. The motif of the Nazirite vow, which has an integral role in the Samson narrative, is not developed at all in the Samuel narrative. Hannah's vow in 1 Sam 1:11 is not referred to again in the whole narrative, nor is there any reference outside the birth narrative that Samuel was a Nazirite. The words ונתתיו ליהוה כל-ימי חייו in v 11 are in fact at variance with the words which occur twice in 1:28 and again in 2:20: וגם אנכי השאלתהו ליהוה כל-הימים אשר היה. If the original vow was to loan the child to Yahweh, it was altered, possibly influenced by an older narrative, to a vow which gave the child to Yahweh.

Further, the textual evidence indicates that the Nazirite vow of Judges 13 has influenced 1 Sam 1:11. Hannah's vow in v 11 reads ונתתיו ליהוה כל-ימי חייו ומורה לא יעלה על-ראשו, "I will give him to the Lord all the days of his life and no razor shall touch his head." The LXX and IQSa[a] include καὶ οἶνον καὶ μέθυσμα οὐ πίεται, "and wine and strong drink I will not drink,"[4] making Hannah's vow the same as the vow of Samson's mother in Judg 13:5.

Hannah's response to Eli's accusation of drunkenness in v 15 also recalls Judg 13:4, 7 and 14. This is particularly significant since the prohibition to the mother of a Nazirite is unknown outside of these two narratives. The

---

[4]See Cross in his translation of Samuel in the NAB.

legal material dealing with Nazirite vows gives the prohibition to the Nazirite himself, never to a parent.[5] The significance of this scene between Eli and Hannah will become clearer when we discuss its function in the narrative.

While it is impossible to prove that the Samuel narrative was originally influenced by the Samson saga, the textual and literary evidence indicates that some influence occurred at a very early stage in the transmission of the tradition.

4. The birth narrative represents a late stage in the history of the Samuel traditions. It was composed after the problems of the monarchy had become apparent, and the life of the last judge had been idealized. It reflects the interests and style of the Dt. historian, although it is not possible to say when it became part of the Deuteronomic history.

Birth narratives are almost always later than stories of heroic deeds, since the interest in the hero's origins does not come until after he has become a significant figure in the history of a people. The birth narrative is usually based on details taken from a hero's life, which are reworked in such a way that foreshadow the deeds and significance of the hero.[6] The details of Samson's birth narrative, particularly the Nazirite vow, are generally interpreted in this way. Early traditions about the source of Samson's strength being in his hair, for example, provide the basis for the later tradition of the Nazirite vow in his birth narrative.[7] Such reinterpretation of early traditions provides the means for redacting ancient Israelite tales of a favorite hero into a unified saga with an explicit theological focus.

---

[5]Num 6:1-21.

[6]See R. E. Brown, *The Birth of the Messiah* (New York: Doubleday, 1977). Although there are important differences between the infancy narratives of the OT and the NT, Brown's method of seeking the origin of the details of the narratives in either the traditions of Jesus' ministry or in the interpretation of an OT tradition is a sound one for any biblical infancy narrative. In OT infancy narratives one must look forward to the traditions of the hero's accomplishments as well as backward to the traditions surrounding earlier heroes. For a different prespective see O. Rank in the classic study, *The Myth of the Birth of the Hero* (New York: Vintage, 1959), 1-96.

[7]See the discussion of the evidence in C. Exum, "Literary Patterns in the Samson Saga," especially 25-36 (unpublished dissertation, Columbia University, 1976). See also J. A. Wharton, "The Secret of Yahweh," Gunkel, *Int* 27 (1973) 48-66, especially 60-61.

The birth narrative of Samuel departs somewhat from this pattern, as it does not appear to incorporate many early traditions about Samuel, but rather is constructed on the basis of a highly developed later picture of Samuel. It does not reinforce the earliest traditions but rather strengthens the later traditions. This is not the birth narrative of an איש אלהים a man of God, or of a ראה a Seer, as Samuel is described in the early traditions of 1 Samuel 9; it is rather a birth narrative which seeks to present Samuel as a judge, priest and prophet. This function is accomplished through the stories of Samuel's childhood: in his favor with Yahweh, in his priestly functions at Shiloh, in his call as a prophet, and in his prophetic announcement to Eli. These childhood narratives are unique to the Samuel infancy narrative; no such stories occur in other OT birth narratives.

The picture of Samuel as prophet, priest and judge is precisely the picture of him which is drawn by the Deuteronomic historian. He is called שפט judge in 1 Sam 7:6, 15-17; 8:1. In 12:11 an interesting textual variant reveals that the tradition of viewing Samuel as a judge in the tradition of the earlier heroes of Israel's tribes continued to develop beyond the Deuteronomic historian. In recounting Israel's history, Samuel names Jerubaal, Barak, Jephthah and Samuel whom Yahweh sent "and delivered you out of the hand of your enemies on every side." The Syriac and the Lucianic LXX read Samson for Samuel, as does Cross in the NAB. Both the nature of the three judges mentioned as well as their historical setting make Samson rather than Samuel more likely as the fourth judge in the original list. There are no early traditions of Samuel as deliverer in the sense that the other three were deliverers. If Samuel has replaced Samson in the list, it is only one example of several of the later tradition which cast Samuel in the model of the earlier charismatic judges.[8]

As in the traditions of the earlier judges, Samuel is credited with subduing the Philistines. He does not accomplish this through military victory, however, but by sacrificing a whole burnt offering and praying to Yahweh. The narrative of Samuel's "victory" over the Philistines in 1 Sam 7:3-17 differs from the stories of the earlier judges in its lack of military details, and in its emphasis on the role which Yahweh played in the victory. It is not the story of Samuel's victory but of Yahweh's. Further, the

---

[8]Schülte goes so far as to say that Samuel is portrayed as the opposite to Samson, and his story is a "Gegengeschichte" which was intended to show the true nature of a holy man. Not the charismatic Samson but the Priestly-prophetic Samuel is the true man of God (pp. 89-90). Hylander, Dus and Press, however, see the Samson tradition as a positive influence on the story of Samuel's birth and childhood.

emphasis is on Samuel's piety rather than his military prowess. The Philistines are routed not by Samuel's military acumen or strength but by his favor with Yahweh. The Deuteronomic redactor is therefore able to evoke the form of the popular judge narratives and yet to use the values of the Deuteronomic historian, in which deliverance is based on obedience and the favor of Yahweh.

The story of Samuel's call as a prophet in 1 Samuel 3 again evokes a Deuteronomic picture of Samuel. It does not reflect the narrative of chapter 9, in which Samuel the Seer is sought by Saul to help locate the lost asses, but rather the tradition of Samuel as prophet in the classical sense, as he appears in 7:3-4, 8:10-18 and 12:6-18.

This picture of Samuel as judge and prophet is the same one which is presented in the birth narrative. The emphasis on Samuel's piety and favor with Yahweh is a significant element in both the birth narrative and the Deuteronomic material about Samuel. This emphasis stands over against the earlier tradition of Samuel as seer and man of God who helps Israel to get her first king. I conclude that the picture of Samuel which emerges from 1 Samuel 1-3 reflects the theological interests of the Deuteronomic historian more accurately than it reflects the historical circumstances of Samuel's boyhood.

But what about the story of Hannah, which is a significant part of the birth narrative? Does this also reflect Deuteronomic theology? The function of the birth narrative is to emphasize the role of Samuel as the last link to the golden age before the monarchy, and the prophet who tried to dissuade Israel from taking the disastrous step of choosing a king. But woven in with the material about the piety of the boy Samuel is the story of the barren mother Hannah. What is the function of the barren mother motif in the Deuteronomic historian's portrait of Samuel?

One of the most striking differences between the birth narrative of Samuel and those of other figures in the Hebrew Bible is the central role which Hannah plays in the story. The importance of the motif of the pious parents was pointed out by Hylander in his classic study of the relation between the Samuel and the Saul traditions.[9] He saw the birth legend not

---

[9]Hylander sees Hannah as "die zugleich kluge und fromme Prophetenmutter," a picture which is developed as a literary device intended to establish the credentials of Samuel. He compares Samuel to Jeremiah (both "cult-prophets"), who was called from his mother's womb. Jer 15:1 refers to Moses and Samuel as the two great prophets (see also Ps 99:6),

as a "pure type" but as a mixture of the two types. One type is the narrative which culminates in the giving of a name; this is represented by the š'l material in the narrative. The other type culminates in the giving of an oracle, and is part of a cultic situation. This second type has dominated the development of the tradition, according to Hylander, and is expressed as a literary tendency in the picture of the "pious mother." This is an important observation, because it recognizes the role of Hannah in the narrative as unusual, and, in fact, foreign to the literary form in which it occurs. Hylander's work, however, is form critical, and he does not probe further into the function of Hannah in the narrative. Since the motif of Hannah's piety is interwoven with the motif of her barrenness, the method of comparative midrash tries to trace the development of these motifs and their function in the Samuel tradition.

The portrait of Hannah in 1 Samuel 1-3 exhibits a different artistic style from the one seen in Genesis and Judges. The differences are striking.

1. While Hannah, like the other mothers, is barren, her desire for a child is expressed more fully and deeply than in the other narratives. The only matriarch whose intense longing for a child was expressed in the narrative is Rachel (Gen 30:1). While it may be in the background, there is no stress on intense longing or suffering in the stories of Sarah, Rebecca or Samson's mother. In 1 Samuel 1, on the other hand, the motifs of Hannah's longing and of her suffering are predominant.

2. Not only does Hannah suffer because of her barrenness, but she suffers reproach and humiliation because of the taunts of Peninnah. She is pictured as the victim of Peninnah's cruelty. When we compare 1 Samuel 1 with the two other stories of the rivalry between a barren and a fruitful wife, we see that the aspect of Hannah as victim is unique to 1 Samuel 1. In the stories of the conflict between Sarah and Hagar and between Rachel and Leah, the beloved but barren wife was not the victim of her child-bearing rival. On the contrary, the high-handed actions of Sarah and Rachel make Hagar the outcast and Leah, the unloved wife, the object of the reader's sympathies. This aspect of the stories is used by the Yahwist to emphasize the importance of Isaac as heir to the promise. Even the question of whether Sarah was right or not is subordinated to the issue of

---

and Hylander argues that the Samuel material was developed under the influence of prophetic traditions. The motif of the clever and pious mother is certainly significant in Exodus 2.

the promise, just as the question of Abraham's morality in Genesis 12 is subordinated to the issue of preserving Sarah and fulfilling the promise. *Errore hominum providentia divina* is a theme on which the Yahwist has many variations.

The motif of rivalry between Hannah and Peninnah, then, is striking, because while it appears to be following the pattern of Genesis 16 and 30, it actually breaks the pattern in an important way. Hannah is neither high-handed nor powerful; her position as the loved wife does not help her. She is rather the victim of Peninnah's taunts and harassment.

3. While Hannah's desire for a child is consuming, she does not devise plans, as Sarah and Rachel did, to circumvent the obstacle of her barrenness. She does what none of the matriarchs did; she simply asks Yahweh for a child.

4. The destiny of the child is determined by Hannah in her vow, rather than by Yahweh. The pattern of a divine annunciation foretelling the nature and destiny of the child to be born, which occurs in the birth narratives of Isaac, Ishmael, Jacob and Samson, is broken here. This is the only birth narrative in which the mother actively determines the role of the child before birth.

5. The portrayal of Hannah's character focuses on her faithfulness and piety. She is pictured as praying, making a vow to Yahweh and finally as fulfilling the vow. Further, the story is set largely at the sanctuary at Shiloh, so that Hannah is seen as a worshipping pilgrim. Reference is made three times to the family making a pilgrimage to Shiloh for the yearly sacrifice (1 Sam 1:3, 21; 2:19). The psalm in chapter 2 is introduced by the words ותתפלל חנה ותאמר "Hannah prayed and said," emphasizing this image of Hannah's piety.

In the differences between the story of Hannah and the stories of other barren women in the Hebrew Bible, two characteristics of Hannah stand out. First, the motif of Hannah as victim of deprivation and humiliation, which is accomplished through the Peninnah material, and secondly, the motif of Hannah as faithful and pious, which is woven through the first two chapters. Both of these motifs provide a clue to the way in which the old tradition of the barren woman is used in 1 Samuel 1-3 and bear close examination.

All of the material about Peninnah and her relationship to Hannah occurs within vv 4-8 of chapter 1. Peninnah and her sons are not mentioned again, although the motif of Hannah's distress does recur. These verses constitute a literary unit; they comprise a little narrative, begin-

Hannah 43

ning in the classic Hebrew narrative style, ויהי היום.[10] The narrative concerns Hannah's place in the family triangle of Elkanah, Hannah and Peninnah. Hans Stoebe, in his commentary on Samuel, refers to the verses as a sentimental expansion which is strongly emotional and non-historical.[11] His reasons for judging them a later addition are literary:

1. The story of the two wives is not developed and does not relate to the historical events in Samuel.
2. The verses are a "long-winded insertion," which do not use the same precision of language evidenced elsewhere in Samuel.
3. The awkward transition from 5b to 6, and the repetition of the phrase יהוה סגר רחמה betrays v 6 as particularly problematic.
4. There is tension between vv 7 and 9. Did Hannah eat at the festival or not?
5. The role of the women in the festival indicates that this material is not contemporary with the time it portrays. The participation of the women presupposes Deut 12:12, 14:26, 15:20 and 16:11.[12]

Stoebe concludes about the verses:

> Inhaltlich freilich ist gerade dieses Stück ein eindrucksvolles Zeugnis für die Stellung der Frau in Israel und ein schönes Beispiel von Gattenliebe und Zartheit. Mit aller Vorsicht lässt sich wohl sagen, dass sich im Gedanklichen eine Verwandtschaft mit Prv. 31:10-31 feststellen lässt.[13]

In comparing these verses with the narratives in Genesis about Sarah-Hagar and Rachel-Leah, which the relationship between Hannah and Peninnah naturally calls to mind, Stoebe concludes that the story of Hannah and Peninnah is different, and ultimately less important:

> Das Motiv der durch Kinderreichtum glücklickeren Nebenbuherlin ist im AT geläufig (Sarah-Hagar; Rahel-Lea), hat

---

[10] See 1 Sam 14:1, 2 Kgs 4:8, Job 1:6; and *GKC* 126s.

[11] Page 96. Stoebe is not alone in viewing the verses as literary rather than historical. It is his dismissal of the scene as simply sentimental which is surprising.

[12] Stoebe assumes that women did not participate in the cult at all until late, but this is by no means certain. See Samuel Terrien, "Toward a Biblical Theology of Womanhood," in *Religion in Life* (1973) 322-333.

[13] *Das Erste Buch Samuelis* 96.

hier aber im Gegensatz zu den gennanten Stellen für die Fortführung der Geschichte keine weitere Bedeutung und erweist sich damit als starker gefühlsmässig betonte Erweiterung.[14]

Stoebe's analysis, while more complete than most commentators', is inadequate because it fails to deal with the final form of 1 Samuel 1. Vv 4-8 present several textual and source critical problems which require more careful attention than Stoebe has given them. More importantly, why are they in the text? If they are an addition, what is their function? To call these verses a sentimental elaboration and a beautiful example of marital love and tenderness does not explain their presence in the present text.

Hylander[15] refers to these verses as "Motivkontamination" and concludes that they function to make Samuel more pious. Pfeiffer refers to the words of harassment as midrash,[16] which are intended to "enhance the picture of historicity" and are "irrelevant." But to dismiss verses because they are not original does violence to the canonical text and therefore to the intentions of the communities in Israel which used the texts and which meditated on them, interpreted them, and above all, let them speak to their needs. Since these communities are ultimately responsible for the preservation and canonization of the Hebrew Bible, it is the responsibility of the exegete to try to discover what meaning an addition or "midrash" had for these communities and why it was preserved as part of the text, rather than scornfully dismiss it. The formation of the text did not stop with the earliest sources, but continued through the modifications made by the communities which used them until the text form was finally fixed.[17]

Before examining the function of the Peninnah material in the infancy narrative of Samuel, we must look at the evidence that these verses are indeed an addition to the original text and particularly at the textual problems which the verses present.

---

[14]Ibid.

[15]*Das Erste Buch Samuelis* 22.

[16]"Midrash in the Books of Samuel" in *Quantulacumque* (ed. R. Casey, S. Lake, A. Lake; London: Christophers, 1937) 303-316.

[17]The ways in which the community used the tradition, whether oral or written, affected the final shape it was to take (indeed, whether it was to survive at all).

Hannah

Verse 5 presents an interesting textual difficulty. What did Elkanah give to Hannah and why? The witnesses read as follows:

MT   ולחנה יתן מנה אחת אפים כי את־חנה
                                              אהב ויהוה סגר רחמה

LXX   καὶ τῇ Αννα ἔδωκεν μερίδα μίαν, ὅτι οὐκ ἦν
        αὐτῇ παιδίον· πλὴν ὅτι τὴν Ανναν ἠγάπα
        Ελκανα ὑπὲρ ταύτην, καὶ κύριος ἀπέκλεισεν
        τὰ περὶ τὴν μήτραν αὐτῆς.

T^J ולחנה יהב חלוק חד בחיר ארי ית
                                     חנה רחים ומן קדם יוי אתמנע מנה ולד

The MT reading of אחת אפים is not intelligible, and there is almost universal agreement to emend the text to אחת אפס כי, following the LXX.

But even with this emendation the problem remains. Did Elkanah give Hannah *only one portion* because she had no child, although he loved her; or did he give her the *best portion* because he loved her, although she had no child? The MT and LXX suggest the first, while the Targum Jonathan clearly says the second. That no solution has been found to this textual problem is clear from the modern translations. The RSV follows the LXX while the NAB follows the Targum (or perhaps an unpublished manuscript from Qumran?). Has the LXX added an emphasis on Hannah's barrenness, or has the Targum softened it? There is simply not enough evidence to decide. The publication of the Qumran Samuel may prove useful in answering these questions.

The LXX text is an especially important witness because it usually renders the MT of Samuel by a slavishly literal translation, even if it does not make sense. The possibility that the LXX represents another *Vorlage* is important and is supported by the evidence from v 6. The references to the harassment of Hannah by Peninnah in vv 6 and 7 are completely absent from the LXX. There is no mention in the LXX of a צרה, a rival wife, nor are the Hebrew verbs וכעסתה and הרעמה represented. Instead, the LXX refers to her θλῖψις and her ἀθυμία τῆς θλίψεως which she suffers.

This is a very different portrait of Hannah from that of the MT. It is a Hannah who is despondent and sorrowing because she has no child, rather than a Hannah who is harassed by her rival wife who has many children.

Similarly, in v 16, Hannah described her actions to Eli as ἐκ πλήθους ἀδολεσχίας μου ἐκτέτακα while in the MT we read כי־מרב שיחי וכעסי

דברתי עד-הנה. Again the LXX makes no reference to Peninnah vexing or tormenting Hannah, while the MT emphasizes it. The Targum Jonathan uses in v 16 the same two verbs which appeared in vv 6-7: אקניותי and וארגזותי.

The tradition about Peninnah's harassment of Hannah now bears closer examination. The words used to express Peninnah's actions are כעסתה and בעבור הרעמה in v 6, and תכעסנה in v 7. Peninnah is described as a צרה in v 6. In v 16 Hannah described her problem as שיחי וכעסי. The most important word is the root כעס used four times. In its verbal form כעס is a trademark of the Deuteronomic historian; of fifty-six occurrences in the Hebrew Bible, twenty are in editorial links of the Deuteronomic historian in Judges and 1 and 2 Kings. Further, twenty-five occurrences are in Jeremiah, Ezekiel, Nehemiah, Chronicles, 3 Isaiah and Qohelet. (The other uses are three times in the Psalter (78, 106 and 112), once in Hosea, three times in Deuteronomy 32 and three times in 1 Samuel 1.) It is clearly a word which was used most often in the sixth century and later, particularly by the Deuteronomic historian. The noun form, used in 1 Sam 1:6 and 16, reflects the same sixth century and later uses. Similarly, the word in verse 16 שיח used with כעס is used often in Job and in the lament Psalms.[18]

The description of Hannah in 1 Samuel 1 seems to echo some of the psalms of individual lament, in which the חסיד cries out to Yahweh in distress. These psalms have several elements in common with each other and with 1 Samuel 1.

Ps 6:7-8

יגעתי באנחתי
אשחה בכל-לילה מטתי בדמעתי ערשי אמסה
עששה מכעס עיני עתקה בכל-צוררי

Ps 31:10-12

חנני יהוה כי צר-לי   עששה בכעס עיני נפשי ובטני
כי כלו ביגון חיי   ושנותי באנחה
כשל בעוני כחי   ועצמי עששו
מכל-צררי   הייתי חרפה ולשכני מאד

---

[18]שיח can also have the meaning of musing or thought, as in 1 Kgs 18:27 or Ps 104:34. It is the use of כעסי parallel to שיחי which shifts its meaning from the neutral ἀδολεσχίας of the LXX to the meaning of complaint.

Besides the use of כעס and צרר, these psalms include the motifs of weeping and of being weak with grief. All of this is echoed in 1 Sam 1:6-8. V 11 of Psalm 31 refers to years spent in sighing; this could be recalled by 1 Sam 1:7; Hannah's distress continued year after year.

I do not suggest that there is a *direct* relationship between 1 Samuel 1 and these psalms of lament; rather that the author (or editor) of 1 Samuel 1-3 was consciously drawing on this tradition of the lament of the *anawim*. He has therefore combined the tradition of the barren women from the patriarchal narratives and the Samson story with the tradition of the righteous man who is in distress and harassed by his adversaries. Or, more precisely, he has reinterpreted the barren matriarch tradition in light of the tradition of the *anawim*. The use of כעס and צרה, words which surely evoked the cry of the defendant in the covenant lawsuit, and of the righteous poor, indicates that the author of Hannah's tale intends more than "a sentimental expansion."

One more problem which requires attention in v 6 is the meaning of the infinitive הרעמה. This is a textual problem; the verb means to thunder and is almost always used to refer to Yahweh thundering on the sea.[19] As this meaning does not make sense in the present context, there have been two approaches to understanding this word.

The first possibility does not emend the text but interprets הרעמה in light of its Aramaic and Mishnaic Hebrew meaning. The causative of רעם often means to murmur or to cause discord. The *ʾaphel* is used in the Targum Onkelos of Num 14:36 to translate וילונו (to murmur against) and the *ʾithpaal* is used in Num 21:5 to translate ידבר. This meaning is understood in a commentary on 1 Sam 1:6 in *Pesikta Rabbati* 2.43: בעבר הרעימה על אלהים לטובתה, "In order to make her murmur against God for her own good."[20] Yalkut Samuel also reflects this meaning, although recognizing the root meaning of "thunder" in order to play on it: "thou makest her thunder against me . . . there are no thunders which are not followed by (fructifying) rain."[21]

However, some of the rabbis apparently did see a problem, for Targum Jonathan reads בדיל לאקניותה "in order to make her jealous," avoiding

---

[19] Except in Ezek 27:35, where it probably means to tremble, because it is used parallel to שערו unless it is emended to דעמו, following the LXX and the Syriac.
[20] See M. Jastrow ספר מלים, 1487.
[21] Ibid.

the root altogether. The use of כעס parallel to קנ׳ is found in Ps 78:58, and this may have influenced the Targum translators.

The second possibility for interpreting רעם is to emend the text to חרפתה. This reflects the reading εξουθενειν which is found in one codex of the LXX and in a reading in the margin of one manuscript of the Vulgate. This emendation is suggested by Kittel in BH^3, and is followed by Cross in the NAB, which reads "Her rival to upset her turned it into a constant reproach to her that the Lord had left her barren." This reading, if correct, may originate in reflection on Gen 30:23, in which Rachel says, "God has taken away my reproach" when Joseph is born to her. As the Hannah material uses the theme of the two wives, it is not impossible that the author intended to evoke the memory of Rachel's reproach when he described Peninnah's treatment of Hannah. The evidence weighs a bit more heavily in favor of this reading, because it is difficult to account for the use of הרעם with the Mishnaic Hebrew meaning of "cause to murmur" in a seventh century text. It is more likely that the text was changed from חרפתה to הרעמה after the meaning of רעם had broadened. However, whether this was a scribal error or an intentional change is impossible to say.

The most striking aspect of v 6, however, is the difference between the LXX and the MT readings. As mentioned above, the LXX has no reference to Peninnah and her harassment of Hannah. The text reads:

ὅτι οὐκ ἔδωκεν αὐτῇ κύριος παιδίον κατὰ τὴν θλῖψιν αὐτῆς καὶ κατὰ τὴν ἀθυμίαν τῆς θλίψεως αὐτῆς, καὶ ἠθύμει διὰ τοῦτο, ὅτι συνέκλεισεν κύριος τὰ περὶ τὴν μήτραν αὐτῆς τοῦ μὴ δοῦναι αὐτῇ παιδίον.

Within the space of vv 5 and 6 the LXX repeats five times that Hannah had no children. The MT mentions it twice, using almost the same phrase both times: סגר יהוה רחמה.

The motif of harassment is continued in the MT in v 7 with the words וכן יעשה שנה בשנה מדי עלתה בבית יהוה כן תכעסנה ותבכה ולא תאכל. Here the words כן תכעסנה appear to be almost a gloss on the words וכן יעשה. The subject is Peninnah, and the object is Hannah. In the LXX, however, the subject is Hannah and the reference is to her despondency and her childlessness. The Targum Jonathan reads כין מרגזא לה "she made her angry." As in v 6, the MT emphasizes Peninnah's active harassment of Hannah, while the LXX does not appear to know this tradition at all. This emphasis on Hannah as victim occurs again in v 16, where Hannah defends herself against Eli with the words כי מרב שיחי וכעסי דברתי

עד-הנה. The LXX, however, reads ὅτι ἐκ πλήθους ἀδολεσχίας μου ἐκτέτακα ἕως νῦν. There is no mention of שיח or כעס, but only of speaking at length. The LXX emphasizes the idea that Yahweh closed Hannah's womb, which was the cause of her distress; the MT, on the other hand, makes Peninnah entirely responsible for Hannah's distress, and emphasizes Hannah's anguish over Peninnah's treatment of her. Has the LXX omitted reference to Peninnah's harassment or has the MT added it? It is probably not so simple; the textual history of Samuel is complex and there were several textual traditions quite early. Pfeiffer, in an article on the midrash in Samuel, has classified 1 Sam 1:6-7 as part of a large collection of midrashic material which came into the text either from the margins of manuscripts or was composed *ad hoc*. In describing the material he says

> It is characteristic of midrashic literature in general to supply picturesque details, which are wholly fictitious, to enhance the appearance of historicity. . . . such irrelevant or circumstantial details are common in the midrash of Samuel.[22]

For Pfeiffer, these historical midrashim contribute nothing to our understanding of the history and literature of ancient Israel, because they are full of misconceptions and blunders. He ends his study with the words

> Its value for us consists chiefly in the information that it furnishes on the early stages of Biblical learnings and interpretation.[23]

But it is precisely in furnishing information about the early stages of interpretation that these "historical midrashim" contribute to our understanding of Israel's history. The work of comparative midrash tries to show that the way in which the community interpreted a text at a particular time provides significant data about the concerns of the community at that time. I will return to this discussion after the textual evidence has been presented.

Verse 11 presents another difference between the MT and the LXX. The LXX lacks the phrase ולא תשכח but reads καὶ μνησθῇς μου. The phrase ולא תשכח following וזכרתני is not surprising and does not add any

---

[22]"Midrash in the Books of Samuel," 310.
[23]Ibid., 316.

new idea to ולא תשכח. However, it is a phrase which is used particularly in community lament psalms, the cry of the *anawim*. In Ps 9:13b-14a we read

לא שכח צעקת עניים
חנני יהוה ראה עניי משנאי

The language of this prayer is close to the language of Hannah's prayer in 1 Sam 1:11. The words לא שכח in the Psalm are almost identical to the words לא תשכח in Hannah's prayer, and ראה עניי is very close to אם-ראה תראה בעני. The same prayer that Yahweh not forget his poor occurs again in Pss 10:12b, 44:25b and 74:19b. The motif of Yahweh remembering his poor is a poignant motif during the Exile and Restoration, and recurs often in the literature of that period. The cry to Yahweh to remember and not forget is especially characteristic of the *anawim*.[24] The absence of the phrase from the LXX and the close resemblance to the language of the laments of the *anawim* make it quite possible that this phrase was added to the Hebrew text from the influence of the community prayers of this group. The addition of this phrase strengthens the identification of Hannah with the *anawim* and, therefore, with Israel in time of oppression and persecution.[25]

The scene of Eli's misunderstanding of Hannah's silent prayer in vv 12-18 also contributes to the picture of Hannah as the victim of unjust harassment. After the author has carefully established Hannah's piety in vv 12-13, Eli's crude attack makes Hannah all the more the object of our sympathies. The literary, almost meditative, nature of the scene is apparent from the language used in it. Hannah's reply to Eli in vv 15-16 is set in the language of the lament psalms, just as her prayer in v 11 was. The

---

[24] See the discussions in Paul van der Berghe, "*'Ani* et *'Anaw* dans les Psaumes*," in *Le Psautier* (ed. R. DeLanghe; Louvain: Publications Universitaires, 1962) 273-295; Leopold Sabourin, *The Psalms* (New York: Alba House, 1974) 95-98; Albert Gelin, *The Poor of Yahweh* (Collegeville, MN: Liturgical, 1964); Martin Dibelius, *James* (Philadelphia: Fortress, 1976) 39-45. Whatever one decides about their origins and identity, the language used to describe them and the lanugage of the prayers is clear.

[25] It is difficult to explain why the phrase would have been dropped from the LXX. Wellhausen, in *Der Text der Bucher Samuelis* (Göttingen: Vandenhoeck & Ruprecht, 1871), suggests that the LXX lacks the phrase possibly because it was offensive ("anstössig," p. 38). If that is the case, Hannah had already by the time of the LXX become highly revered.

phrase ואשפך את־נפשי is reminiscent of Ps 42:5, ואשפכה עלי נפשי, Ps 102:1, ישפך שיחו and Ps 142:3, אשפך לפניו שיחי.

The use of שיחי in Hannah's response in v 16 is especially significant. It occurs in two of the laments, above, as well as in Pss 55:3 and 64:2 and seven times in Job. It is interpreted in v 16 by the word כעס used already three times in vv 6-7. In the LXX text of v 16, שיחי is translated by ἀδολεσχίας, a word which reflects the meaning of concerns or words rather than complaints. The word וכעסי is not represented in the LXX, just as it was not represented in the LXX text of vv 6-7.

Hannah uses the language of the psalmist in lament, particularly the language of the *anawim*. Psalm 42, already cited, is especially striking in this regard, as the reference to Hannah's weeping and rejection of food in v 8 is almost a narrative expansion on Ps 42:4:

היתה־לי דמעתי לחם   יומם ולילה

The phrase וכעסתה צרתה גם־כעס בעבור הרעמה in v 6 could well be a reflection of Ps 42:11

ברצח בעצמותי   חרפוני צוררי

The picture of Hannah at prayer, then, appears to have been influenced by the tradition of the lament psalm. This is not an historical account of the birth of Samuel, not is it a sentimental or heroic elaboration; it is rather a story resignified for Israel in persecution, a story of the faithful remnant who put their trust in Yahweh and are finally vindicated.

The textual evidence indicates that the tradition preserved in the MT has been created by glosses in vv 6, 7, 11 and 16, which emphasize Peninnah's cruelty and Hannah's piety and distress. The little narrative in vv 4-8 probably is, as Stoebe and others suggested, an addition to the original birth narrative. However, far from being irrelevant or extraneous, these verses, along with vv 11 and 16, establish the basis for a new theological interpretation of the old story.

Hannah's Psalm in 2:1-11 is almost universally recognized as a late addition to the story. Certainly its references to the king indicate that it is not from the period of Samuel's youth; further, the use of the psalms anachronistically in narratives is now recognized as a literary device and it is not necessary to demonstrate that Hannah could not have spoken the Psalm.[26] It is necessary, however, to indicate the significance of the Psalm, for it is still dismissed as not relevant to the birth narrative

---

[26]See the work of R. A. Carlson, *David, the Chosen King* (Stockholm: Almqvist & Wiksell, 1964), on the Deuteronomic redactors' use of traditional psalms, especially 45-46.

because it is a late addition. But it is precisely because it is a late addition that the Psalm is significant, for it defines the canonical shape of the tradition of Samuel's birth. The Psalm gives us a glimpse into Israelite hermeneutics—it allows us to see how the birth narrative was interpreted and contemporized by the community in a period when the national pride which had originally shaped the story had been crushed. The ability of the prophets to re-interpret the old Canaanite and Babylonian mythological motifs has been recognized and appreciated, but the creativity represented in the several stages of growth of the birth narrative has not been well recognized, though it is part of the same gift of adaptability which was the lifeblood of Israel.[27]

R. A. Carlson, in his excellent study of the tradition history of 2 Samuel, has shown the relationships between Deuteronomy 32, 2 Sam 22-23:7 and 1 Sam 2:1-10. These psalms are all part of the shaping of the older Davidic materials by the Deuteronomic redactors (referred to as the D-Group by Carlson), and they function as theological interpretations of the narratives which precede them, as well as foreshadowings of what follows. Particularly useful is Carlson's demonstration of the ways in

---

[27] But see the excellent study of Joseph Bourke, "Samuel and the Ark: A Study on Contrasts," *Dominican Studies* 7 (1954) 73-103. Bourke sees the infancy narrative of Samuel as the work of an Ephraimite author who has re-worked old traditions about Samuel's birth into a formal structure, in which there is a symmetrical balance between the scenes and a clear contrast between good and evil and between oppressor and oppressed. The characters are stylized into traditional literary types; Samuel and Hannah are the *anawim* while Eli and his sons and Peninnah are the *poʿale awen*. The end of Hannah's barrenness foreshadows the end of the period of barrenness in Israel during Eli's priesthood. It is not simply the story of Samuel's birth but of the triumph of good over evil.

It is quite possible that this interpretation was given the story at the earliest stage of its written history, as Bourke suggests. However, the textual history of 1 Samuel 1-2 indicates that the process of interpreting Hannah as one of the *anawim* continued and intensified with the Deuteronomic redactors. Our textual study suggested that the Peninnah material of 1:6 was not original but added. The lateness of the language (even Bourke's parallels are late) supports this thesis, as pointed out above. More interesting is the connection between the infancy narrative and the story of the ark; Bourke shows how the themes of the infancy narrative are elaborated on a national scale in the history of the ark and the anointing of Saul.

which the D-Group used catchwords and leitmotifs to link the Psalms with the narrative, and to tie the narrative elements to each other.

Carlson relates Hannah's song especially to 1 Sam 2:27-36, the prophecy of the man of God foretelling the fall of the house of Eli. The words "Those who are full hire themselves out for bread . . ." in Hannah's song echo the prophecy in 2:36: ". . . and everyone who is left in your house should come to implore him for a piece of silver or a loaf of bread, and shall say, 'Put me, I pray you, in one of the priest's places, that I may eat a morsel of bread.'" Similarly, the last words of the Psalm, ". . . he will give strength to his king, and exalt the power of his anointed" are linked with 2:35, "And I will raise up for myself a faithful priest . . . and he shall go in and out before my anointed for ever."

> The associative connexion of 2:1-10 with 2:27-36 and the figure of Samuel gives a direct indication of the general thematic function of this psalm in the narrative of 1-2 Sam. It is perfectly evident that Hannah's song of praise is a Deuteronomic insertion into the web of tradition, intended to deepen the ideological interpretation of the events described in 1-2 Sam. From the point of view of the nature of God—Yahweh as high god, "the Rock" and "the Most High" (v. 2, 10)—it is significant that it corresponds both to its counterpart in 2 Sam. 22 and to Deut. 32-33; all these passages have been incorporated by the D-group.[28]

Carlson's analysis of the editorial methods of the D-group is helpful, and the link between Hannah's song and the prophecy of Eli's fall explains in part the function of the psalm. However, as Carlson points out, the associative technique of the D-group recapitulates as well as foreshadows; the psalms interpret the narrative material which precedes them as well as looking ahead. But what interpretation does the psalm give to 1 Samuel 1-2, and whose interpretation is it?

Hertzberg concludes that the psalm lends added support to the increasingly idealistic picture of Samuel. "The psalm puts the birth, and hence the life of Samuel in the context of the all-powerful saving acts of God."[29] This understanding of the function of the psalm presupposes that the narrative is intended primarily to present Samuel as favored by Yahweh even before birth. While this may have been intended at one stage

---

[28]Carlson, *David, The Chosen King*, 45-46.
[29]*I and II Samuel*, 31.

of the birth narrative, it is probably not the focus of the narrative in its final form. The key catchword in the psalm is in v 5: "The barren has borne seven"; this phrase links the psalm to Hannah. But the catchword often does more than simply link literary units; it provides a clue to the theme of the piece.

The emphasis in the birth narrative has been shifted from Samuel to Hannah, at least in 1-2:10. Whatever significance the birth narrative of Samuel had in its earlier forms, whether as a Shiloh tradition, a legend of the birth of Saul, a demonstration of Samuel's favor with Yahweh or of the downfall of Eli, in its final form it has a meaning which is defined by Hannah's barrenness, her distress and her vindication by Yahweh. The psalm does not relate to Samuel or to his role as judge and prophet, and it relates only partially to the fall of Eli and the rise of Zadok; it does refer again and again to the downtrodden and the poor. The psalm functions, then, to dramatize Hannah as the symbol of the *anawim*, the poor of Yahweh. If the reader missed the significance of Hannah's barrenness and affliction in the narrative, the editor has insured that it will not escape him after the psalm. *The psalm functions to interpret the meaning of the narrative.* It is the editor's way of answering the question, "How are we to read this story?" The psalm provides the hermeneutic context in which to hear the story of Hannah and Peninnah. Because of the psalm, Hannah is not simply the mother of Samuel, but becomes a symbol of the graciousness of Yahweh to his faithful ones, particularly to Israel in time of affliction. By placing the psalm on Hannah's lips the editors have generalized Hannah's experience of deprivation, sorrow and finally vindication. The despair she feels in her barrenness and the bitterness she knows because of Peninnah's taunts must have been poignantly shared by a people who themselves felt barren, forsaken and bitter. Hannah is no longer simply the mother of Samuel, but she is one of the *Hasidim* (2:9) whom Yahweh has delivered. His gift of Samuel to Hannah in her deprivation is seen as a kind of down payment on his gift of restoration to his destitute people, a sign of his graciousness which he had performed of old and would perform again.

Our analysis of the first part of the birth narrative of Samuel indicates redaction which has shifted the focus from Samuel to Hannah. What can be said about the provenance of this redaction and its relation to the earlier materials? Robert Pfeiffer, in a study of the midrashim in Samuel cited above, suggests three stages in the editing of an original work composed in the tenth century:

1. Between 750 and 550 the work was "supplemented at various times with stories and speeches of diverse origin."[30] 1 Samuel 1, which Pfeiffer calls a haggadic legend, represents the best of these additions, and he dates it before 650. Included in this group are also 1 Sam 2:11-26 and 3; the purpose of these is the vilification of Eli.

2. In ca. 550 the Deuteronomic editors completed their edition of Samuel, but it was "perfunctory," with few additions and changes.

3. After the canonization of the Pentateuch around 400, study and annotation of the Books of Samuel became significant, and many annotations crept into the text, both from the margins and by *ad hoc* compositions. Pfeiffer characterizes these additions as useless and tendentious. Among these additions he includes 1 Sam 1:6-7 and 2:1-10 and the prophecy against Eli in 2:27-36.

While Pfeiffer's stages are useful for showing the long history and diversity of the text of Samuel, his dating of passages is less helpful. Carlson's work on the psalms in Samuel is able to explain how the psalms reflect the Deuteronomic historian's compositional techniques as well as theology; this is more persuasive than Pfeiffer's suggestion that they are part of the "miscellaneous material" which came into the text between 400 and 200 B.C.E. The importance of the written Torah after ca. 444 B.C.E. must have given fresh impetus to the study of Samuel, as well as other prophetic books, as Pfeiffer notes (though for him this study resulted in corruption of the text), and it is not impossible that a few phrases in 1 Samuel 1-2 are from this period. The literary evidence indicates, however, that the final shaping of the story and the addition of the psalm are part of a careful and deliberate work, which was completed in the early post-exilic period. Pfeiffer has underestimated the contribution of the Deuteronomic historian.[31] Far from a perfunctory editing of Samuel, they were able to reshape the older work to speak to the new crisis in Israel. 1 Samuel 1-3 foreshadows the beginning of a new age in Israel, an age of Zadokites rather than Aaronides, of Yahweh's anointed one, and of the deliverance of the faithful ones. The editors were not negating the earlier meanings of the story but were adding another level of meaning, so that it would speak anew to their community.

---

[30]Pfeiffer, "Midrash in the Books of Samuel," 304.

[31]For the stages of editing encompassed by the term Deuteronomic historian, see F. M. Cross, *Canaanite Myth and Hebrew Epic* (Cambridge: Harvard University, 1973) 274-289.

The story of Hannah adds a new dimension to the theology of the Deuteronomic historian and indicates a more complex situation than a simple obedience-brings-blessing and disobedience-brings-curse theology. Hannah's troubles are nowhere attributed to any sin or wrongdoing, either by her or her family; her barrenness and her harrassment are simply given as unexplained suffering. The barrenness can be understood as a means of linking Samuel to the traditions of the Patriarchs, and of underlining his favor with Yahweh, but Hannah's suffering because of Peninnah does not reflect any earlier tradition. Her torment is simply a given; it is innocent suffering, and it is described and drawn out at length and in detail. Indeed, it is the injustice of Hannah's suffering which is at the heart of the story. In the psalm also those who are suffering are set over against the wicked; they suffer injustice and are finally vindicated by Yahweh. The addition of the psalm indicates that the redactors are calling our attention to this aspect of suffering and vindication, an aspect which is not found in the earlier stories of barren mothers, at least not in such bold relief. The theme of Hannah as one of the faithful ones, one who is victim of her adversary yet remains steadfast in her faith in Yahweh and is ultimately rewarded by him, is the creation of the Deuteronomic historian. It is his "midrash" on the barren matriarch tradition. But it is not a midrash in Pfeiffer's sense of a corruption and falsification of the text; it is midrash in the sense of interpretation of a normative tradition for the sake of the community which has preserved the tradition.[32] This new use of the tradition of the barren mother, which made the old story of Samuel's birth into a story of hope for Israel in exile, was to alter the shape of the barren matriarch tradition permanently.

THE FUNCTION OF THE MOTIF

The motif of the barren mother functions differently in the story of Hannah from the way it functioned in the Torah. While for the Yahwist the motif demonstrated Yahweh's power over fertility and underlined grace as the primary force by which Israel lived, for the author of 1 Samuel 1-3 these functions are present but secondary. The primary interest in Hannah is twofold. First, she sets Samuel in continuity with the Patriarchs and therefore with the old order (i.e., before the monarchy).

---

[32]Roger le Déaut, "Apropos A Definition of Midrash," *Int* 25 (1971) 259-282, especially 275: "It is above all for the benefit of the community that the comtemporary meaning of the Word of God is sought."

Hannah   57

Samuel is surrounded by the aura of authority and antiquity by his birth narrative. Secondly, Hannah functions as a symbol of a group, perhaps even as Israel herself. The matriarchs in Genesis were not symbols of a community; they were distinct individuals whose significance lay in their stories. But Hannah is a type of the *anawim;* she is faithful and pious, yet suffering. She functions not primarily as mother but as one who has been rescued by Yahweh. Her story gives graphic and poignant content to the Psalms of lament and gives concrete meaning to the affirmation that Yahweh raises the lowly and rewards his righteous ones. Hannah is more truly the mother of Israel than Sarah, for in the figure of the poor one of low estate who was visited and remembered by Yahweh Israel could see herself.

THE METHODS OF THE EDITOR

The author of the story has used the same theological principle as the Yahwist—that which is despised by men is looked upon with favor by Yahweh and used for his purposes—but it has been used in a new way. The author of 1 Samuel 1-3 has applied the tradition of the barren woman to a new context: the identity of a whole people. He has used an individual to stand for the whole people; he has generalized the story of a barren woman who bears a son from an individual to a people.

Further, the author has provided the interpretation of his story as a part of the story. The Psalm functions as a "gloss" on the story; it insures that the main point of the story will be heard.

But a more subtle hermeneutic is also at work. While the Yahwist emphasized the pregnancies of the matriarchs as a result purely of Yahweh's graciousness (he insures that they cannot be seen as being rewarded by omitting mention of piousness, good deeds or prayer; further he seems to take delight in describing their *lack* of faith), the author of Hannah's story interprets her pregnancy as a result of her relationship with Yahweh. Samuel was an answer to her prayers and the response of Yahweh to her affliction; he was the reward which Yahweh gave to his faithful one.

These two changes in the tradition—the use of the woman as a symbol of the whole people and the birth of the child as a response to prayer and faithfulness—represent a real departure from the Yahwist's stories and were to become the basis for all further interpretations of the barren matriarch stories.

3
Sing, O Barren One

The next stage in the development of the barren matriarch tradition presents a remarkable example of how creatively Israel's early traditions were reflected upon and reshaped before the emergence of classical midrash. A brief review of what we have seen so far will prepare the way for this new stage. Three points from the preceding chapters are particularly salient:

1. The tradition of the barren woman who bore a son was already, in its earliest form in the Hebrew Bible, the result of reflection upon an old narrative in the light of the Yahwist's theology of history and the needs of the nation as he saw them in the tenth century. The similarity of the stories of Sarah, Rachel, Rebecca, Samson's mother, and Hannah is not a coincidence; rather all of these narratives have been consciously related to each other and to a common motif.

2. All of the barren matriarch material occurs in the same literary form, that of the birth narrative.

3. The story of Hannah, while using the Pentateuchal traditions about the barren woman, breaks the pattern in significant ways, especially in the use of poetry to interpret the narrative and the interpretation of Hannah's experience as a paradigm for Israel's experience.

The use of the barren matriarch as a symbol of the people rather than simply an individual woman, which underlies 1 Samuel 1-3, is developed to its fullest expression in Second Isaiah. Here the creative genius of Second Isaiah and the experience of the Exile together gave rise to a new form of the barren matriarch tradition, one that was loosed from the historical moorings of the Bronze Age and which became the basis for all further use of the tradition. How has this transformation occurred? What were Second Isaiah's hermeneutics as he interpreted the ancient traditions about Sarah? The texts in which the tradition of the barren woman is used are Isa 49:19-21, 51:1-3, and 54:1-3. It is immediately apparent that this motif does not play a major role in Second Isaiah; the texts are few and short. Yet this resignification of the tradition would provide one of the central motifs by which Israel defined herself in the formative Second Temple period.

Isa 51:2 is the only explicit reference to Sarah outside of the Pentateuch. The text is a reflection on the story of the call of Abraham and the birth of Isaac in light of the subsequent history of Israel. Sarah is here called the mother not of Isaac but of all who seek Yahweh. The plural suffix of the verb תחוללכם underlines that Sarah bore not one son, Isaac, but many sons, who became Israel. Already in the sixth century the idea that the true sons of Abraham are those who seek Yahweh anticipates the later Pauline concept of sons according to the flesh as against sons according to the promise. Israel's identity as sons of Abraham cannot be simply claimed; it must be lived out in the Covenant.

Isaiah's use of the second person plural throughout this passage emphasizes the link between Israel's past and her present. This is a remarkable passage, for it reveals that Isaiah interpreted the story of Sarah using hermeneutical priniciples which are characteristic of a later period. For Isaiah the importance of the Torah story was not so much in the Bronze Age, when Isaac was born, as in the present, when the sons of Abraham and Sarah are struggling to understand the devastation which has come upon them. It must have been this kind of attitude toward the traditions and this kind of reflection on them which provided the impetus for the redaction of the Pentateuch.[1] When Israel was reduced to an insignificant band of exiles, the old stories about the Patriarchs who were few in number took on a new meaning. This kind of interpretation, which takes the present or the future as the most important referent of the text, is characteristic of Second Temple exegesis and of later rabbinic exegesis.[2]

---

[1] See J. A. Sanders, *Torah and Canon* (Philadelphia: Fortress, 1972), and "Adaptable for Life: The Nature and Function of Canon," *Magnalia Dei: The Mighty Acts of God. Essays on the Bible and Archaeology in Memory of G. Ernest Wright* (ed. F. M. Cross and W. E. Lemke and P. D. Miller; Garden City: Doubleday, 1976) 531-560.

[2] See Renée Bloch's seminal article, "Midrash," in the *DBSup* 5, cols. 1263-81. An English translation by the present writer can be found in *Approaches to Early Judaism: Theory and Practice* (ed. William S. Green; Missoula: Scholars, 1978) 29-53. See also Daniel Patte, *Early Jewish Hermeneutic in Palestine* (Missoula: Scholars, 1975) 76-81. Actualization characterized exegesis at Qumran, in the Targums and in the NT and, to a lesser extent, in some rabbinic exegesis.

This most fundamental hermeneutical principle of the Second Temple period is anticipated by Second Isaiah in his use of the tradition of Sarah as the wife of Abraham and mother of Isaac.

The reference to the rock and the pit is puzzling. Some attempts have been made to interpret the rock as Yahweh, by emending the verbs to the active voice, following the LXX,[3] but the parallelism of the verse suggests rather that the rock is Abraham and the pit is Sarah. More likely is the suggestion of Paul Volz that Second Isaiah is alluding to the ancient mythological belief that men were born from a rock or drawn out of a cave, a belief which was part of the Semitic mythology of the chthonian mother goddess.[4] Second Isaiah's frequent use of mythological motifs, particularly creation myths, supports this view. Deut 32:18 shows that this belief in the birth of man from a rock was known in Israel and assimilated into Yahwism: צור ילדך תשי ותשכח אל מחללך Jer 2:27 indicates that the ancient belief in the rock was popular in the sixth century. אמרים לעץ אבי אתה ולאבן את ילדתני.

In alluding to this ancient birth tradition Isaiah presents Abraham and Sarah as the Adam and Eve of Israel. As Westermann notes, "He wishes to give Israel's descent from Abraham and Sarah the status of an act of creation, on a par with D-I's description of the nation's election at the exodus as creation."[5] Westermann, however, loses the full force of the creation image, because he rearranges the text, separating v 3 from v 2. But the reference to the *Urzeit* in v 3 is part of the "midrashic" reflection on Sarah and Abraham. Israel is to reflect on her creation: just as God created her out of Abraham and Sarah in the beginning, so he will create her anew out of a few exiles. Just as the first couple lived in the garden of the gods, so will Yahweh restore Zion to be again like Eden. The reference to the Garden of Eden in v 3 follows logically on the reference to creation in v 2.

Isaiah has apparently combined two traditions: an ancient mythological tradition about the birth of the first man and the historical tradition about the birth of Isaac. The result of this conflation is the image of the creation of Israel from the first parents, at the time of the creation of the world. By moving Abraham and Sarah out of their historical setting in the Bronze Age into the *Urzeit*, Isaiah has indeed given Israel's beginning the status of an act of creation. In Second Isaiah the *Urzeit* is the

---

[3]P. A. H. de Boer, *Second Isaiah's Message* (Leiden: Brill, 1956) 58-63.
[4]Paul Volz, *Jesaia II* (Leipzig: A. Beichertsche, 1932) 109-112.
[5]Claus Westermann, *Isaiah 40-66* (Philadelphia: Westminster, 1966) 236.

paradigm for the *Endzeit:* the creation of old is paralleled and surpassed by the new creation which Yahweh is about to accomplish.⁶ In moving the parenthood of Abraham and Sarah to the primeval time Second Isaiah was able to use them in his motif of first creation and new creation. The way in which Yahweh called the single man Abraham and made him a nation, and chose the barren Sarah to become the mother of all Israel is the paradigm for the way in which he will recreate the nation out of the desolate band of exiles which is now Israel. Second Isaiah was able to accomplish this new understanding of Sarah's maternity by combining a mythological tradition from Israel's neighbors with an ancient patriarchal tradition from Israel's past. This uniting of mythological and historical motifs is characteristic of Isaiah and is one of the techniques by which he reinterprets traditional material to speak in a new situation.

By reinterpreting Sarah the mother of Isaac into Sarah the mother of Israel, Isaiah appears to be answering a question of identity which had arisen in his community. The context suggests that the question which the prophet was addressing was that of the exiles who asked Ezekiel, "How then shall we live?" (Ezek 33:10). Isaiah answers their question with a story—the story of how a nation came from an old man and a barren woman provided the answer to the question of how Israel could live.⁷

Sarah and Jerusalem

רני עקרה לא ילדה   פצחי רנה וצהלי לא-חלה
כי-רבים בני-שוממה   מבני בעולה אמר יהוה
הרחיבי מקום אהלך   ויריעות משכנותיך יטו   אל-תחשכי
האריכי מיתריך   ויתדתיך חזקי
כי ימין ושמאול תפרצי   וזרעך גוים יירש
וערים נשמות יושיבו

---

⁶This is clear in such passages as Isa 51:9-11, in which the mythological battle with the sea is united with the historical memory of the Exodus to describe Yahweh's power over chaos and the way in which Yahweh will overcome the chaos of the exile and lead Israel out of bondage again. For a discussion of *Urzeit* and *Endzeit* see Brevard Childs, *Myth and Reality in the Old Testament* (London: SCM, 1968) 73-84.

⁷See J. A. Sanders, "Hermeneutics in True and False Prophecy," *Canon and Authority* (ed. G. W. Coats and Burke O. Long; Philadelphia: Fortress, 1977) 21-41, especially section IV.

Sing, O Barren One

> Sing, o barren one, who did not bear;
> break forth into singing and cry aloud,
> you who have not been in travail!
> For the children of the desolate one
> will be more than the children of her
>   that is married, says the Lord.
> Enlarge the place of your tent,
> and let the curtains of your habitations
>   be stretched out;
> hold not back, lengthen your cords
> and strengthen your stakes.
> For you will spread abroad to the right and
>   to the left,
> and your descendants will possess the nations
> and will people the desolate cities.
>
> Isa 54:1-3

    The brevity of this passage is significant because it reflects a change in the literary form in which the barren matriarch tradition occurs. For the first time, there is no birth narrative into which the story of the barren woman is set; there is rather an oracle of salvation addressed to the woman herself. This change from narrative to poetry has two significant effects on the material. First, the text no longer speaks about the woman in the third person, but now uses the second person and addresses her directly. The entire focus of the barren matriarch tradition has shifted from the birth narrative of a special child to an oracle addressed to the mother. I have tried to show already how the final form of Samuel's birth narrative has prepared the groundwork for such a shift, particularly in the use of the psalm, which focuses attention on the mother. However, because that narrative was developed out of an earlier birth narrative (whether of Saul or Samuel) the basic outlines of the birth narrative are still present and functional in the text, and the child Samuel is the focus of the story. But that narrative, in fact, stretched the genre of birth narrative to its limits, so fully did it develop the characters of both mother and child. Isaiah's message will not fit the birth narrative mold; it exceeds the limits of even the amplified form in 1 Samuel 1-3.

    Isaiah is the first to pour the ancient tradition into a new mold, and this mold has radically transformed the tradition from a story about the birth of a child to the story of the birth of a people.

    The second significant effect of the change in literary form is the shift from telling a story about the past to foretelling a story about the future.

While the birth narratives told the personal history of Israel's heroes, Isaiah's oracles proclaim the future of the people Israel. The difference is not reflected simply by the use of the imperfect rather than the perfect, or of poetry rather than prose, but it is reflected by the change from narrative to proclamation. The change in literary form is significant because it signals that the old material is being used with a new purpose: it is to proclaim what is coming rather than to relate the past.

Finally, literary form has affected the old material by making it general rather than individual. The barren one in Isaiah 54 is not named, though it is clearly Zion, as she is called in 49:19-21. The barren woman is not a particular woman of history but Zion, who is a figure for the whole people Israel. Nor are the children who will be born to her named; they too are symbolic rather than particular. The poetic form has allowed Isaiah to reinterpret the barren Sarah as the barren Zion, the people Israel. By freeing the tradition from its Bronze Age context and from its relation to particular women, Isaiah has transformed it into a symbol, a symbol which could speak poignantly of both Israel's past and her future.

If the literary form has allowed Isaiah to transform the ancient tradition, the content of the oracles keeps the reader immersed in the roots of that tradition. Each passage is a pastiche of Bronze Age traditions woven together with Isaianic interpretations of them. This method of alluding to ancient traditions and then interpreting them in new language is one of the hallmarks of Second Isaiah, as we have already seen, and it bears a close resemblance to the biblical interpretations of the Second Temple period, particularly the anthological style.[8] While Second Isaiah's use of the traditions of creation and exodus are universally recognized, his use of the traditions of the barren women have been only superficially noted. Yet the development of the tradition of Zion as the mother of the new people of God, which has such wide and important uses in the Second Temple period, originates in Second Isaiah's use of the barren matriarch tradition.

These verses probably constitute an independent oracle.[9] The change in v 4 to the metaphors of Zion as the divorced wife who is taken back, and the command אל-תיראי suggest that two independent oracles have been linked together. The figure of Zion as the woman whom Yahweh loves, whether as a barren woman who is part of his plan for Israel, or as the

---

[8]A. Robert, "Littéraires (Genres)," *DBSup* 5, col. 411.

[9]Volz, 130-132. Westermann, 270-273, does not separate vv 4-10 from vv 1-3.

unfaithful wife whom he still loves, provides the unifying motif. The *Stichwörter* are שוממה "desolate" in v 1 and אלמנותיך "widowhood" in v 4; in both passages Yahweh transforms the bereft and desolate woman into one over whom the entire community rejoices.

Just as in 51:2 Second Isaiah interpreted the story of Sarah by means of an ancient mythological tradition about the birth of mankind from a rock, so in 54:1-3 he interprets the story of Sarah's barrenness by means of the tradition which personified Jerusalem as feminine and as the wife of the deity. The frequent and varied ways in which Second Isaiah described Zion as feminine indicate that he was using a tradition which was well known and understood in sixth century Judah. This is not simply a poetic metaphor for Jerusalem, but is rather another ancient mythological motif which he has taken over and "Israelitized."[10] What did the figure of Jerusalem as a woman signify to the community which Second Isaiah addressed in the sixth century B.C.E.?

The figure of Jerusalem as feminine was probably inherited by the Israelites when they took over the ancient Jebusite capital city. It was part of the West Semitic mythology to view capital cities as goddesses and to give such cities titles which were also used for goddesses.[11] The cities are referred to as *btwlt* "virgin" and *bt* "daughter," just as Anath is called *btwlt ʿnt*. Ugarit itself is called *bt ugrt*, "daughter Ugarit,"[12] and Babylon is named בתולת בת-בבל "virgin daughter Babylon" in Isa 47:1.[13] Similarly, cities bear the title אם "mother," as in 2 Sam 20:19 and implied in Num 21:25. Like the goddess Anath, the city is both virgin and mother; the virginity signifies youth and beauty while the maternity signifies fecundity.[14] The goddess who is represented by the city is married to the deity who is patron of the city; sometimes the name of the city is simply

---

[10]See Sanders, "Adaptable for Life," 541.

[11]For the full arguments and evidence see Aloysius Fitzgerald, "The Mythological Background for the Presentation of Jerusalem as a Queen and False Worship as Adultery in the OT," *CBQ* 34 (1972) 403-416; and "*BTWLT* and *BT* as Titles for Capital Cities," *CBQ* 37 (1975) 167-83.

[12]Cited in Richard E. Whitaker, *A Concordance of the Ugaritic Literature* (Cambridge: Harvard, 1972) 154.

[13]W. F. Stinespring has shown that בת-ציון is an appositional rather than a possessive genitive. The translation "daughter of Zion" is misleading, as it suggests in English that Zion had a daughter; the meaning of the term is that Zion is herself a daughter, i.e., feminine. See "No Daughter of Zion," *Encounter* 26 (1965) 133-41.

[14]Anath is both virgin and wife of Baal; see, for example, *ANET*, 142.

a feminine form of the god's name, as in בעלות, Bealoth.[15] In fact, the doctrine of the inviolability of Jerusalem, which predates David's capture of the city, may originate in the belief in the city as a goddess protected by her patron Deity.[16]

Many of the Jebusite cultic and mythic traditions surrounding the city were adopted by the Israelites with only superficial changes,[17] and it is not unlikely that the concept of Jerusalem as a queen, bride and mother was also taken over. It was not until the eighth century, however, that the image of the city as goddess took on a distinctly Israelite form and a truly new stage in the history of the tradition began. It was probably Hosea who first took the bold step of making the ancient mythology explicit by describing Israel as the wife of Yahweh. Here the entire land, not simply the capital city, is personified as the woman who is married to the god. Hos 2:1, ולא-תקראי-לי עוד בעלי indicates that a tradition of the land as the spouse of Baal already existed; Hosea was not simply using poetic license, but was reinterpreting an ancient Canaanite tradition.

It is interesting that the ancient Canaanite tradition became monotheistic and Israelite only when its Canaanite form was fully expressed. Hosea did not simply use the traditional titles for cities; he portrayed the marriage between the land and her divine spouse, just as Canaanite mythology had done. The idea of a cultic marriage between Israel and Yahweh could never originate within Yahwism, but a Canaanite cultic image of the city as a goddess married to her patron god could easily be made to serve the covenant theology of the prophets. The Canaanite image allowed Hosea to speak of the relation between Israel and Yahweh with an intensity which was new in the literature of Israel, and he was able to portray her apostasy with a poignancy which had not been known before in Israel's sacred traditions. Because the marriage between Israel and Yahweh was not seen as merely a figure of speech, but had its basis in a cultic tradition, it was particularly effective in expressing the passion of Yahweh for Israel and the effects of her apostasy.[18]

The community which Second Isaiah addressed, then, knew the tradition of Jerusalem, and of the whole people, described as a woman. It was by joining this tradition with the Torah story of the barren matriarchs that

---

[15] Fitzgerald, "Mythological Background," 411.
[16] Ibid., 415. See also Samuel Terrien, "The Omphalos Myth and Hebrew Religion," *VT* 20 (1970) 315-338.
[17] Terrien gives several convincing examples.
[18] See, for example, Isa 1:21, Jer 2:1-3:5, Ezekiel 16 and 23.

Sing, O Barren One

Second Isaiah produced the image of Jerusalem as the barren woman who would bear many sons, an image which was to endure into the first century C.E.

The first verse of Isaiah 54 illustrates how well Second Isaiah re-told the ancient traditions in a new context and used them to interpret a new situation. The use of the imperative רני parallel with פצחי indicates a hymn of praise as in 44:23:

רנו שמים כי-עשה יהוה   הריעו תחתיות ארץ   פצחו הרים רנה

and in 49:13:

רנו שמים וגילי ארץ   יפצחו הרים רנה

But while here nature is being called on to witness God's salvation and to be the choir for the thanksgiving service, in 54:1-3 it is the one being saved who is called on to rejoice. Not the cosmos, but the barren one, is asked to sing. The words עקרה לא ילדה specifically recall the matriarchs of Genesis. עקרה is used of Sarah in Gen 11:30, of Rebecca in Gen 25:21 and of Rachel in Gen 29:31. The phrase לא ילדה described Sarah in Gen 16:1 and Rachel in Gen 30:1. The conflation of these two phrases לא עקרה ילדה occurs in Judg 13:2, 3, in a description of Samson's mother. Second Isaiah's use of the phrase עקרה לא ילדה would recall the old stories of the barren matriarchs to the consciousness of his community, just as his references to treks through the desert led by Yahweh would recall the old exodus traditions to them.

The parallel term in 54:1, לא-חלה is not from the patriarchal traditions, but is a later, poetic word for giving birth, and means literally to be in labor. It is used in 51:2 specifically of Sarah as the one who gave birth to the people Israel: הביטו אל-אברהם אביכם ואל-שרה תחוללכם Isaiah has established already in the first stich the recollection of the barren matriarchs and the expectation of a new birth announcement.

The second stich gives the cause for singing:

כי-רבים בני-שוממה   מבני בעולה אמר יהוה

The joyful news is not simply that a barren woman will give birth to a son, but that the barren woman will have more sons than the woman who is married. The comparison between the two women, one barren and one with children, recalls the motif of rivalry between the two wives. We have seen how this motif, used first of Sarah and Hagar, became attached to the motif of the barren woman so that the stories of Rachel and Hannah were modeled on the rivalry between Sarah and Hagar. Second Isaiah is not only announcing the birth of a son to a barren woman; he is also announcing the vindication of the devastated and captive people over their enemy. But in setting the woman who is שוממה over against her who is בעולה, Second Isaiah has reinterpreted the tradition. The contrast in the Torah story is not between a woman who is desolate and one who is married, but between a woman who is barren and one who is fruitful. What is the meaning of the contrast between שוממה and בעולה?

The same image occurs in Isa 62:4: לא יאמר לך עוד עזובה ולארצך לא-יאמר עוד שממה. Isaiah uses the term שממה of the land in 49:8, 19 and in 61:4 as well as in 62:4 to describe the holocaust of Jerusalem in 586 B.C.E. The contrast between שממה and בעולה occurs in Isa 62:4 כי-חפץ יהוה בך וארצך תבעל. The prophet uses the image of a woman in disgrace contrasted with a woman in her glory, as a bride, to describe the change that Yahweh is about to make in Jerusalem. שוממה is a word which is used almost exclusively in the literature of the exile to describe the land and the people. The only pre-exilic use attested is in 2 Sam 13:20: ותשב תמר ושוממה בית אבשלום אחיה. This passage is instructive, for it indicates that when שוממה was applied to a woman, it was a *terminus technicus* which referred to her status in the community. A woman was marriageable only as a virgin; therefore, a man who raped a virgin was required by Israelite law to marry her.[19] Amnon's rape of Tamar destroyed her virginity, that for which the bride-price was paid, yet as her half-brother, he could not marry her.[20] She was therefore defiled, not marriageable, and would live out her days in solitude, without husband or children. The story of Jephthah's daughter in Judg 11:29-40 tells poignantly of the devastation of a woman who had to die childless, and the description of the daughter and her companions bewailing her virginity in solitude in the mountains before her death indicates that such a status was almost equivalent to death in Israel, and like death, it was accompanied by its own rites of mourning. Tamar, likewise, mourns the loss of her virginity and her fate as one who would die childless. 2 Sam 13:19 described her actions of mourning: covering her head with ashes, rending her special virgin's robe, and wailing. She was שוממה, as one who is dead.

Almost all of the exilic uses of the term שוממה occur in images of sexual disgrace, always of Jerusalem personified as a woman. The

---

[19] Deut 22:28-29; Exod 22:16-17.
[20] Lev 18:9.

technical nature of the term was apparently known to the exilic prophets, who use it frequently to describe the devastation of Jerusalem.

The outrageous nature of the situation now becomes clear: Yahweh has taken for his wife a woman whose defilement could never be purified to make her marriageable; her position was defined as שוממה and she was as one who is dead. To hear the words חפץ and בעל replacing שוממה must have jarred in the ears of Second Isaiah's audience, for she who was untouchable is now called by names of most intimate endearment. Second Isaiah has reminded his community of the old stories of the rivalry between the barren and the fruitful wives and how Yahweh visited the barren one to give her a son. But he then reinterprets the old story: what he did for Sarah and for Rachel who were barren was only done in days of old; now he is taking to himself Jerusalem, who is שוממה.

> Enlarge the place of your tent,
>   and let the curtains of your habitations
>   be stretched out;
> hold not back, lengthen your cords
>   and strengthen your stakes.
> For you will spread abroad
>   to the right and to the left,
>   and your descendants will possess the nations
>   and will people the desolate cities.
>
> Isa 54:2-3

If the language of the first part of the passage has alluded to Yahweh's choice of the barren woman over the fruitful one and of the ruined woman over the married one, the second part recalls his choice of a family which was nomadic, small and powerless. The grammatical structure of the two parts is identical: a series of imperatives followed by a כי clause which explains the reason for the commands. The command to enlarge the tent is detailed by the technical terms: משכנותיך, מיתריך and יתדתיך. The use of these terms evokes the semi-nomadic life of the patriarchs in the Bronze Age, and makes the allusion to patriarchal times very graphic. Of course the image of Israel living in tents would be especially poignant to the exiles whom Second Isaiah addressed, as they had been uprooted suddenly from comfortable houses in cities to the homeless and uncertain life of exile. The allusion to the unsettled life of the patriarchs was therefore a reminder of the present condition of the people and addressed the question of whether Israel in exile was still Israel.

The climax of the passage comes in verse 3, which recalls the promise of land and descendants given to the patriarchs and renews that promise for the present generation of Abraham's descendants. The phrase כי-ימין ושמאול תפרצי is an allusion to the promise; it is particularly reminiscent of the promise to Jacob in Gen 28:14:

והיה זרעך כעפר הארץ   ופרצת ימה וקדמה וצפנה ונגבה

The last two stichoi are commentary on the promise in light of Israel's present condition. The form is almost that of the pesher of Qumran, or of the homiletic exegesis of the rabbis. Second Isaiah says: "The promise to our fathers was that their descendants would spread abroad. The meaning of that promise is this: the ruined city of Jerusalem will be repopulated so that there will hardly be room for everyone, and the sons born to Zion now will inherit the land. The fulfillment of that promise to our fathers will be seen by this generation." This is the technique of Second Isaiah throughout this passage, and indeed in other places where he uses Bronze Age traditions. He begins in language which is traditional and reminiscent of the Torah traditions, and then switches to language which is contemporary, using words which are exilic or post-exilic.

THE FUNCTION OF THE TRADITION IN SECOND ISAIAH

The use of a well known patriarchal motif gave authority to the prophet's words. Just as his appeal to the ancient creation and exodus traditions lent authority to his prophecy that the captive Judahites would return home, so his appeal to the barren matriarch tradition gave authority to his words of comfort which said that the people would be built up again. J. A. Sanders has demonstrated the prophetic use of Torah traditions as "references of authority";[21] that these traditions had a special status in Israel by the eighth century has been well attested.[22] The Judahites should know that their present devastated condition was not an obstacle for Yahweh; the story of how he had overcome Sarah's barrenness was evidence of that.

---

[21]"Hermeneutics in True and False Prophecy," 31.
[22]See, for example, G. von Rad, *Old Testament Theology* (New York: Harper and Row, 1965) 2 99-119.

PROPHETIC HERMENEUTICS

What were the principles by which Second Isaiah interpreted the ancient story of the birth of Isaac? First, Second Isaiah assumes a kind of typology. The creation of Israel out of Sarah's barren womb is paradigmatic for the new creation of Israel out of the desolate Jerusalem; for Second Isaiah one might almost say that this creation was pre-figured in the birth of Isaac. The authoritative tradition becomes a valid "interpreter" of the present situation; hence Sarah is almost a "type" for Jerusalem. This principle can be seen most clearly in Second Isaiah's use of the creation and exodus traditions, and it anticipates the hermeneutic of typology which was to become so important in early Jewish exegesis.

But it was not only his "typological" interpretation of the Torah tradition which characterized Second Isaiah's hermeneutics. In a study of the hermeneutics of true and false prophecy, J. A. Sanders has contrasted Second Isaiah's use of the tradition of Sarah and Abraham with that of some of the sanguine inhabitants left in Jerusalem a few months after its fall.[23] Ezekiel rejected their interpretation that if God had given the land to Abraham, who was one man, then he would surely give it to them, who were many. They thought that Yahweh would be consistent by giving again as he had given at first. Ezekiel responded by rejecting their interpretation of Abraham's story and their notion of consistency. Just as he had made known at first that he was Yahweh by the giving of the land, so now he was making known that he was Yahweh by the destruction of the land. For Ezekiel, their interptetation of the story of Abraham was providing false hope and obscuring the meaning of the destruction of Jerusalem, and he countered it with words of judgment.

But in Second Isaiah's community the situation was different; the exiles had despaired of ever being the people Israel again and they were assimilating into Babylonian culture.

> The challenge they apparently needed to retain their Jewish identity amounted to a symphony of consolation, which Deutero-Isaiah nonetheless intimately related to God's judgments of fifty years earlier.[24]

---

[23]"Hermeneutics in True and False Prophecy," 31-33.
[24]Ibid., 33.

Why was the people's use of the Abraham story in Ezekiel's time "false," while in Second Isaiah's time basically the same use of the story was "true"? The true prophet, like Yahweh, is always out ahead of his people. While they are amassing armies and assuring themselves of Yahweh's aid, the prophet is announcing complete destruction. But when they have been devastated and conclude that Yahweh has abandoned them, or worse, has been defeated himself, the prophet announces that Yahweh was visiting Jerusalem just as he had visited Sarah. The same principle is illustrated in Jeremiah; he breaks the clay pot and announces the destruction of Jerusalem while the inhabitants prepare for victory, but when Nebuchadnezzar's army is overrunning the city, he purchases a piece of property within the city, at the point when it was worthless because it was about to be seized by the Babylonians.[25] The historical context in which a tradition is cited (or a prophetic sign acted out) itself functions as a kind of hermeneutical principle.

Another factor which distinguishes Second Isaiah's use of the story of Abraham and Sarah from that of the people in Ezek 33:23-30 is that of selective emphasis. The latter cited the gift of the land to Abraham, while Second Isaiah cited the gift of children to Sarah. By this emphasis on Sarah, Second Isaiah reinterpreted the promise in a way which must have appeared radical to his hearers: the fulfillment of the promise to Abraham is not in the giving of the land, but in the making of a people. A woman can give birth anywhere; Yahweh can build up his people wherever a contemporary Sarah and Abraham are living. The reference to tent dwelling in Isa 54:2 is also part of this focus on the people rather than the land. While the return to the land is very important for Second Isaiah, his emphasis on Sarah as mother rather than on Abraham as land-owner indicates that for him the identity of the exiles as children of the promise obtained in Babylon, and that this identity was the crucial portion of the promise to remember.

---

[25] See Jeremiah 19 and 32 for the story of the broken flask and the purchase of the field.

4

Jerusalem Our Mother

THE FEMININE IN ISRAELITE THEOLOGY

Before pursuing the development of Second Isaiah's image of Jerusalem, it will be helpful to pause and ask how a feminine religious image was able to function for a community in which such imagery was very rare. How were the prophet's words, describing Yahweh's salvation in such feminine and sexual terms, heard by his audience? What was the context in which he preached such words?

Yahwism was a religion with very little feminine religious imagery.[1] If the religion of Israel was to be truly monotheistic, an idea which was embraced by only a minority of the people, deities of Israel's neighbors could have no role in Israel's faith. But while the characteristics of the male deities could be incorporated into Israel's description of Yahweh, the characteristics of the female deities for the most part could not. The insistence on defining Yahweh over against fertility rites and the deification of sexuality which characterized Semitic religion meant that Yahweh was neither masculine nor feminine, but transcended sexuality. He was the Lord of fertility and he had created sexuality, but he did not participate in it himself.

In popular religion, however, this translated to a god without a consort. If fertility is guaranteed by ritual re-enactment on earth of the sexual union of the gods and their consorts, the denial of a consort for Yahweh put his power over fertility in doubt and thereby placed the fertility of the earth, animals and women in jeopardy. The feminine functions of pregnancy, childbirth and nursing were viewed with awe in the ancient world and were seen not as gifts of the gods but as participation in the

---

[1] For some exceptions see Phyllis Trible, "Depatriarchalizing in Biblical Tradition," *JAAR*, 51/1 (March 1973) 30-48, and *God and the Rhetoric of Sexuality* (Philadelphia: Fortress, 1978).

divine nature.² The act of giving birth was viewed as a manifestation of divine power and was therefore mysterious, dangerous and awesome.

Genesis 2-3 is an example of an attempt to demythologize the feminine power of giving birth. The curious story of woman coming from man rather than man being born from woman uses ancient mythological motifs in the service of a new theological statement: it was not a mother goddess, but the living power of Yahweh which brought man into being. The motif of the rib, echoing the Sumerian goddess of life, "the Lady of the Rib," and the naming of the woman חוה with its interpretation as "the mother of all living," indicate that the woman once played a more significant role in the story of the creation of man.³ For the Yahwist's audience in the tenth century the message that woman is not a representative of the mother goddess but is rather an עזר כנגדו must have been startling. The very presence of such a text in the literature of ancient Israel indicates that the deification of the feminine was a problem in the Yahwistic religion.

In every period of Israel's history there were goddesses whose popularity and influence could not be completely eradicated by the prophets or by the official Yahwistic cultus. Whether it was Ashera, the magna mater, Ishtar or the Queen of Heaven, the struggle against the feminine deities was constant and difficult. The vast number of terra cotta figurines with protuberant bellies and prominent breasts which have been found at sites all over Israel bears witness to the deep need of the ancient Israelites to incorporate the feminine principle into their religious expression.⁴

---

²See, for example, the Enuma Elish, in which sexuality is pre-existent and sexual union begins the process of creation. In Genesis 1, on the other hand, sexuality is created by God and has no role in his creative powers.

³See the very interesting study of John A. Bailey, "Initiation and the Primal Woman in Gilgamesh and Genesis 2-3," *JBL* 89 (1970) 137-150. The psychoanalytic approach of Theodor Reik in *The Creation of Woman* (New York: McGraw-Hill, 1960) is informed by history of religions studies and is of some use.

⁴J. B. Pritchard, *Palestinian Figurines* (New Haven: American Oriental Society, 1943); *The Ancient Near East in Pictures Relating to the Old Testament* (Princeton: University Press, 1959); *The Ancient Near East: Supplementary Texts and Pictures Relating to the Old Testament* (Princeton: University Press, 1969); *The Bronze Age Cemetery at Gibeon* (Philadelphia: University of Pennsylvania Museum, 1963); Eric Neumann, *The Great Mother* (Princeton: University Press, 1963); Raphael Patai, *The Hebrew Goddess* (New York: Ktav, 1967).

While the insistence that mother goddesses and fertility rites had no place in Israel's religion was quite appropriate and necessary in the struggle against assimilation to the surrounding cultures, paradoxically the absence of the feminine in "orthodox" Yahwism caused the Israelites to seek it in heterodox ways. In light of the historical evidence, it is difficult to see how monotheism could be solidly established in Israel before aceptable feminine imagery was incorporated into the religion. The failure of the people to accept Yahweh as the God who could be both masculine and feminine is thoroughly documented in the Hebrew Bible.[5]

The figure of Hochma in Prov 8:22-31 is an interesting exception to the veto of feminine religious imagery. While this tradition is not developed in the literature of the Hebrew Bible, it receives extensive development in the literature of Second Temple Judaism.[6] The very context of the Hymn to Wisdom, and the personification of Wisdom as the alluring and gracious teacher in Proverbs 1-9, underscore the struggle between monotheistic Yahwism and the cults of the various goddesses which occurred in ancient Israel. Lady Wisdom is set over against Lady Folly אשת כסילות; young men are invited by חכמה to learn the ways that lead to life, and beckoned by נכריה to her house whose paths lead to Sheol. In the context of Proverbs 1-9 at least, the feminine figure of חכמה appears to be presented as a competitive alternative to the cult of the "foreign woman," the cultic prostitute.

As long as the battle with Canaanite and the Babylonian religions continued and the monotheistic character of Yahwism was in doubt, the feminine principle represented the cults of goddesses and could not be tolerated in the religion of Yahweh. The prophets, at least, made that clear.

It is interesting that with the emergence of monotheistic Yahwism after the Exile (what Morton Smith calls the triumph of the Yahweh-alone

---

[5]The cycle of installing images of Ashera in the Temple and purging the Temple of these images reported in 2 Kings is evidence. As late as after the fall of Jerusalem the Judahites were still worshipping the "Queen of Heaven"—Jer 44:15-19.

[6]For a discussion of the problems, see McKane, *Proverbs*. The theory originated with G. Boström, *Proverbiastudien: Die Weisheit und das Fremde Weib in Spr. 1-9* (Lund, 1935). R. N. Whybray in *Wisdom in Proverbs* argues against the mythological interpretation.

For the relation between Wisdom and Isis see Hans Conzelmann, "The Mother of Wisdom," in *The Future of Our Religious Past* (ed., J. M. Robinson; New York, 1971).

party)[7] and weakening of the threat of the cults of Semitic goddesses, feminine imagery is given free expression and begins to flower in early Judaism. The figure of Hochma becomes prominent in the literature of the Second Temple period. She is described in increasingly feminine and sexual language; the Greek version of Prov 8:22-31, Sir 51:13-30 and its Hebrew recension from Cave 11 at Qumran[8] all illustrate the willingness of early Jewish theologians to use feminine religious imagery in significant ways.

Besides Hochma, the image of the Shekinah, the presence of God as an independent feminine being, begins to be developed[9] along with the image of the Torah as feminine.[10] The sudden plethora of feminine imagery in a religious context from which it had been rejected for so long suggests that the threat which feminine imagery had originally posed was lost in the transition from Israelite religion to early Judaism.

It is significant that it was precisely in the transition from the religion of Israel to early Judaism that the status of women changed for the worse. Samuel Terrien, in two articles which contribute valuable insights to the study of women and of feminine imagery in Israel,[11] suggests why the post-exilic period was a turning point in the status of women. Two factors were apparently at work: the concern for ritual purity and the desire for racial purity.

The concern for ritual purity is illustrated by the emphasis on sin as ritual impurity, used extensively by Ezekiel. The priestly laws of purity, given new importance by their position in the written Torah, intended to guard the community against ritual pollution. The very identity of the community was as a people holy to Yahweh, which in priestly thinking meant not only separate to Yahweh, but also in a state of ritual purity. Contact with women was an ever-present source of ritual defilement; the

---

[7] Morton Smith, *Palestinian Parties and Politics That Shaped the Old Testament* (New York: Columbia University Press, 1971) chaps. V and VI.

[8] J. A. Sanders, *The Dead Sea Psalms Scroll* (Ithaca: Cornell, 1971) 112-117.

[9] The term appears first in the Targums, especially in Onkelos, as a circumlocution for the divine name.

[10] For references to the haggadic use of these concepts, a useful collection is Montefiore and Lowe, A *Rabbinic Anthology* (New York: Schocken, 1974).

[11] Samuel Terrien, "The Omphalos Myth and Hebrew Religion," *VT* 20 (1970) 315-338, and "Toward a Biblical Theology of Womanhood," *Religion in Life* (1973) 322-333.

freedom of women had therefore to be limited to protect the community from ritual impurity.

The concern for racial purity arose out of the fear of some of the small band of returning Judahites that their identity would be lost through assimilation with the foreigners who lived around Jerusalem. The legislation which required the exiles to "put away" their foreign wives and their children (Ezra 10:1-44 and Neh 13:23-30) implied, Terrien says, "the superiority of religious collective concerns over the respect for the individual feminine personality."[12]

In the period of the beginnings of Judaism, then, two attitudes toward the feminine coexisted. On the one hand, women were viewed as a source of ritual impurity which needed to be carefully regulated; on the other hand, feminine imagery became an increasingly important part of the spiritual vocabulary of Second Temple Judaism. This curious pairing of attitudes, which began during the post-exilic struggle for preservation and identity, became characteristic of rabbinic Judaism. Perhaps when the boundaries were so carefully drawn around feminine sexuality it did not pose an imminent threat to the community, and a naturally rich source of poetic and religious metaphor was thereby freed from the arena of taboo and made available to the arena of the sacred. In any case, the sudden flowering of feminine religious imagery during the Second Temple period suggests that a tendency which had long been present in Israel but which could not be expressed had finally come to fruition.

ZION AS MOTHER IN ISAIAH 56-66

The author of Isaiah 56-66 was responsible for developing the feminine imagery of Zion beyond the Pentateuchal tradition of the barren matriarchs. In Isa 66:7-14 the prophet has drawn upon Second Isaiah's image of Jerusalem as a mother giving birth to a new people, but he has changed the image from a barren woman made fruitful to a loving mother drawing her children to herself. What is the function of this very physical feminine imagery of the mother nursing her children in the prophecy of Isaiah 56-66?

Claus Westermann[13] refers to v 11 as an "overdrawing of imagery" which is typical of Third Isaiah, particularly in images of abundance. But Westermann's aesthetic judgment does not explain how the prophet's

---

[12]"The Omphalos Myth," 337, n. 2.
[13]*Isaiah 40-66* (Philadelphia: Westminster, 1969) 420.

words would have sounded to his audience. The power of the post-exilic prophetic words was not in their eccentricity, but in their basis in Israel's traditions. The only real source of authority for Third Isaiah was tradition, and he called freely upon the traditions of the Pentateuch and upon Second Isaiah's interpretations of them. But what tradition is behind the image of Zion as mother who provides all of her children with food and comfort from her own body?

The historial context of the passage is the experience of discouragement which overtook the exiles after the first return to Judah in 538 B.C.E. The birth of sons to Jerusalem in Isa 49:19-21 and 54:1-3 is now doubted; the returning exiles are few and the task of rebuilding the city is overwhelming. In Isa 66:9 the prophet directly addresses the problem with the image of Yahweh as one who completes his work; he does not abandon the woman in labor, but remains with her and causes the child to be born.

It is in vv 10-12, however, that the prophet developes the figures of Zion as the nurturing and comforting mother:

שמחו את-ירושלם וגילו בה כל-אהביה
שישו אתה משוש כל-המתאבלים עליה
למען תינקו ושבעתם משד תנחמיה
למען תמצו והתענגתם מזיז כבודה
כי-כה אמר יהוה הנני נטה-אליה כנהר שלום
וכנחל שוטף כבוד גוים
וינקתם על-צד תנשאו ועל-ברכים תשעשעו

The description of Zion as nursing mother recalls Isa 49:22-23:

והביאו בניך בחצן ובנתיך על-כתף תנשאנה
והיו מלכים אמניך ושרותיהם מיניקתיך

But Second Isaiah does not describe Zion as nursing; it is the foreigners who serve as wet nurses and guardians for Zion's children, at Yahweh's command. While in Second Isaiah Zion is the recipient of Yahweh's fruitfulness and bounty, in Isaiah 56-66 it is Zion herself who is the source of well-being and abundant food. Zion has changed from the desolate woman who is redeemed by Yahweh to the all-sufficient mother whose abundance provides comfort and nourishment.

The language of Isa 66:10-12 does not describe a human mother feeding her baby but suggests a deity feeding her people. The word התענג is used by both Second Isaiah and Isaiah 56-66 to indicate delight which comes from Yahweh (58:14, 55:2). Compare Isa 55:2: למה תשקלו-כסף בלוא-לחם

Jerusalem Our Mother

ויגיעכם בלוא לשבעה   שמעו שמוע אלי ואכלו-טוב   ותתענג בדשן נפשכם
with 66:11:

למען תינקו ושבעתם   משד תנחמיה
למען תמצו והתענגתם   מזיז כבודה

The same words, שבע, be satisfied, and התענג, take delight in, describe Yahweh's feast of wine and milk, in 55:1-2 and Zion's breasts full of milk in 66:11. Her breasts give comfort; this is the only time in Second Isaiah or Isaiah 56-66 that comfort is given by anyone other than Yahweh (see Isa 12:1, 40:1, 49:13, 51:3, 12, 52:9, 57:18). Zion is described as performing functions which are elsewhere attributed to the deity. The popularity of this image of Zion as nursing mother is attested by its occurrence in the literature of Qumran. In a Apostrophe to Zion, Isa 66:10-11 is woven into a text in which the poet remembers and celebrates Zion as the mother of the future generations of Israel.[14]

This image of Zion giving birth miraculously and feeding her children from her own abundance is reminiscent of the ancient Semitic mother goddess, whose cult had never completely disappeared from Israel. The emphasis on Zion's breasts would not have been missed by the prophet's audience, who still remembered, and in some cases still possessed, figurines of the mother goddess holding her breasts in a gesture of invitation and of self-glorification. Terrien's study of the Jebusite myth of Jerusalem as the navel of the earth and the central site of the cult of the Magna Mater in her chthonian aspect has demonstrated the significance of the Semitic Earth Mother for the Jerusalem cult. The adoration of the Terra Mater, Terrien shows, was part of the official Temple cultus during most of the divided Monarchy.

The ancient Jebusite omphalos myth became slowly transformed into a Zion theology which was acceptable in Yahwism. Many elements of the old mythology can be seen in the prophetic and poetic images of Zion as the resting place of Yahweh, as the place from which mankind originated, and as the heavenly city.[15] It is, as Childs has said, the mythic space.[16]

The distinctively feminine aspects of the Jebusite mythology were either demythologized and purged of sexual connotations, or they were part of the illicit practices which plagued the Temple worship and were

---

[14]The full text is in Sanders, *The Dead Sea Psalms Scroll*, 123.
[15]E.g., in 4 Ezra 10:25-49 and Revelation 21.
[16]Brevard Childs, *Myth and Reality* (London: SCM, 1960) 84-94.

rooted out by the reforms of Hezekiah and Josiah, only to return in even more blatant forms.[17] In this context the use of the Jebusite tradition in Third Isaiah accomplished the first successful adaptation of the Magna Mater image to Yahwism. The ancient link of Jerusalem with the great mother is recalled by Third Isaiah and for the first time it is in the service of monotheistic Yahwism rather than in conflict with it.

THE FUNCTION OF THE IMAGE

While Second Isaiah's use of the Jerusalem-as-woman tradition functioned to interpret the ancient Torah story about Sarah, Third Isaiah's use of the tradition has a very different function. It is not the relation to the Torah story which interests Third Isaiah, but rather the development of an independent tradition of Zion as mother of the exiles. This image of Zion functions in two ways.

First, it provides a feminine religious image which is consistent with monotheistic Yahwism. Zion, described as the Tellus Mater, the earth mother who gives birth to her people and nourishes them from her own fertility and abundance, presents an acceptable form of the mother goddess. The development of such a significant and acceptable feminine religious image was important for the survival of monotheistic Yahwism, as we have tried to show above.

Secondly, and probably more significant in the immediate historical context in which Third Isaiah lived, was the function of Zion as she who could unite the scattered and broken-hearted exiles. The question of identity was the crucial one for them: could Israel still exist? Who now were the people of the covenant? Could these uprooted and dispersed exiles still be one people, or ought they to assimilate to the land in which they lived and let Israel die? For Third Isaiah the answer was clear: the scattered people were brothers and sisters, all children of one mother, who was Zion. As life had been given by Yahweh through Sarah so long ago, it was being given by him again through Zion.

Third Isaiah alludes to the ancient tradition of Zion as the center of the earth, which in Second Isaiah became the place to which the whole world would gather to see the salvation of Yahweh. But the Zion of Third Isaiah is not simply the physical space; he has recaptured the ancient *idea* of

---

[17]Hezekiah removes the bronze serpent (2 Kgs 18:4); Manassah rebuilds altars and places images of Ashera in Temple (2 Kgs 21:1-9); Josiah removes Ashera from Temple (2 Kgs 23:6).

Zion. The mother Zion of Third Isaiah is a religious idea which functions to give a common identity to the exiles. While the exiles certainly longed to return to their homeland, nevertheless the idea of Zion as their mother could transcend the physical land and give them a common identity even when the land was devastated. The weight of tradition, which had developed in Israel since the time of the first adoption of Jebusite tradition and cultus, had already surrounded Jerusalem with a religious significance which exceeded the purely physical aspects of land. With Third Isaiah the significance of Jerusalem as a physical reality is beginning to give way to the new significance of Jerusalem as a religious idea, a spiritual reality whose importance does not depend on the physical land. The physical land is still important for Third Isaiah, but because the function of his Mother Zion is not as a place but as a person, the development toward the Jewish doctrine of the heavenly Zion has already begun.

JERUSALEM AS MOTHER IN THE BOOK OF BARUCH

In the apocryphal book of Baruch (second century B.C.E.),[18] the images of Jerusalem as mother comforting her children and as desolate woman comforted by God are used in a collection of poems of comfort. The text borrows freely from Isaiah and shares its eschatological setting, but it is clearly derivative and lacks the mythic dimensions which make the Isaiah texts so rich.

Jerusalem speaks in the first person, mourning her children and then speaking to them to comfort them. This is not Jerusalem the mother like Sarah or Jerusalem the Magna Mater; it is a literary device which makes Jerusalem the mouthpiece of the poet. "I was left desolate because of the sins of my children, because they turned away from the law of God" (4:12). Through the device of Jerusalem the mother the poet explains why the devastation of the Exile has occurred.

The poet recalls another of the mothers of Israel: the image of Rachel weeping for her children in Jer 31:15:

> A voice is heard in Ramah,
> lamentation and bitter weeping.

---

[18]For introductory questions see the article of A. Fitzgerald in *JBC* (Englewood Cliffs: Prentice Hall, 1968) 614-619, and Emanuel Tov, *The Book of Baruch, also called I Baruch* (Greek and Hebrew) (Missoula: Scholars, 1975).

> Rachel is weeping for her children;
> she refuses to be comforted for her children,
> because they are not.[19]

The author of Baruch pictures Jerusalem, like Rachel, in weeping and sorrow for her children (4:11), left desolate without her sons (4:12, 16, 19), and mourning without comfort (4:20). This conflation of the images of Jerusalem from Jeremiah and Isaiah becomes standard in the early Jewish literature. With the Jews in exile and the city destroyed, Jerusalem is like Rachel weeping for her children; when the Jews return, Jerusalem will be like Sarah giving birth, or like the bride whom Yahweh takes back to himself.

The author of Baruch uses the image of mother Jerusalem to instruct the exiles that the same God who punished them will also deliver them. She tells them, "Take courage, my children, cry to God, and he will deliver you from the power and hand of the enemy" (4:21), and "For he who brought these calamities upon you will deliver you from the hand of your enemies" (4:18).

In using the prophetic image of Jerusalem as feminine, the author of this passage has also absorbed the prophetic point that it is the same Yahweh who sends away and who brings back, who brings disasters and who delivers from disaster. The author of this passage has incorporated the prophetic idea that the experience of the Exile is part of Yahweh's plan for Israel. The message of comfort is not primarily the promise of restoration but the knowledge that the suffering of the people is not meaningless and is in the control of Yahweh.

While Jerusalem is presented as the mother of the exiles and the bride of Yahweh in the prophetic tradition, she speaks like the figure of Wisdom in Proverbs 1-9. Her words are words of instruction, the advice of the wise woman to her children. Like Wisdom she teaches the young that they will find life with Yahweh if they attend to her. As Wisdom is contrasted with Folly, Jerusalem is contrasted with the city which received the exiles, personified as a woman who will be destroyed.

The similarity between the figure of Jerusalem and of Wisdom in this text is emphasized by the context. The poem about Jerusalem is preceded by a hymn to Wisdom (Bar 3:9-4:4). The two poems were edited together

---

[19]On Jeremiah's image see Phyllis Trible, "The Gift of A Poem: A Rhetorical Study of Jeremiah 31:15-22," *ANQ* 17 (March 1977) 271-80, and *God and the Rhetoric of Sexuality*, 39-53.

in the second century B.C.E. with no redactional links or comments. It is the feminine figures of Wisdom and Jerusalem which provide the unifying motif of the poems, and it is these figures which function as the *Stichmotiv* for two otherwise unrelated poems.

The anthological style of the poems about Jerusalem, in which Isaiah 40-66 is freely drawn upon and alluded to, is evidence not only that the authority of an older tradition is assumed, but also that the feminine images of Jerusalem had become established. By the second century B.C.E. apparently the image of Jerusalem as mother had become as acceptable as the figure of Lady Wisdom, and, in fact, had taken on some of her characteristics. This could only have happened if the Isaian image had met a need in the Jewish community. For the image to be preserved as part of the prophetic corpus indicates the accepted authority of the prophet; for the image to be expanded and developed signifies that it had both stability and was truly canonical.

JERUSALEM AS MOTHER IN 4 EZRA

The Ezra Apocalypse is a first century C.E. Jewish work, the heart of which is the recounting of the seven visions of the seer Salathiel, who is identified with Ezra in order to lend authority to the work. It is extant only in Latin, Syriac and Ethiopic translations, made presumably from the Greek which came from the original Hebrew and Aramaic.[20] In its present form it contains a Christian introduction (chaps. 1-2) and conclusion (chaps. 15-16), but the visions were addressed to the problem of the fall of Jerusalem in 70 C.E. and the persecution of the Jews by Rome.

In the fourth vision, 4 Ezra 9:26-10:59, the seer Salathiel is sent by the angel Uriel to the field of Ardat, where he sees a woman in mourning. He asks her why she is weeping and she tells her story:

> I, thy servant, was barren, and bore no child, though I had a husband thirty years. Both hourly and daily during these thirty years I besought the Most High night and day. And it came to pass after thirty years God heard thy handmaid and looked

---

[20] R. H. Charles, *The Apocrypha and Pseudepigrapha of the Old Testament* (trans. E. H. Box; Oxford: Clarendon, 1913) 2, 541-552; see now also Jacob Myers, *I and II Esdras: Introduction, Translation and Commentary* (Garden City: Doubleday, 1974) 275-280. For general bibliography on the work see James H. Charlesworth, *The Pseudepigrapha and Modern Research* (Missoula: Scholars, 1976) 111-116.

upon my affliction; He considered my distress, and gave me a son. And I rejoiced greatly, I and my husband and all my fellow-townsfolk, and we gave great glory unto the Mighty One. And I reared him with great travail. So when he was grown up, I came to take him a wife, and made a feast day.

And it came to pass when my son entered into his wedding chamber, he fell down and died. Then I removed the lights, and all my fellow-townsfolk rose up to comfort me; but I remained quiet until the night of the next day. And it came to pass when they were all quiet (and desisted) from consoling, as I remained quiet, I rose up by night, and fled, and came to this field, as thou seest. And I purpose never again to return to the city, but here to stay and neither eat nor drink but continually to mourn and to fast till I die.[21]

Salathiel answers her angrily:

O thou above all other women most foolish! Seest thou not our mourning, and what has befallen us? How Sion, the mother of us all is in great grief and deep affliction?

He continues, describing the defilement and destruction of the Temple in 70 C.E., and telling the woman to stop mourning, as it is Sion who has cause to mourn. While he talks with her she is transformed:

And it came to pass, while I was talking to her, lo! her countenance on a sudden shone exceedingly, and her aspect became brilliant as lightning, so that I was too much afraid: and while I was debating what this might mean, she suddenly uttered a loud and fearful cry, so that the earth shook at the noise. And when I looked, lo! the woman was no longer visible to me, but there was a City builded, and a place shewed itself of large foundations.

Salathiel cries out for Uriel, who appears and interprets the vision to him:

The woman who appeared to thee a little while ago, whom thou sawest mourning and begannest to comfort: whereas now thou seest no likeness of a woman any more, but a builded City hath appeared unto thee: and whereas she told thee of the misfortune of her son—this is the interpretation: This

---

[21] G. H. Box, *The Ezra Apocalypse* (London: Pittman, 1912) 221.

> woman, whom thou sawest is Sion, whom thou now beholdest as a builded City. And whereas she said unto thee that she was barren thirty years: the reason is that there were three thousand years in the world before any offering was offered in it. And it came to pass after three thousand years that Solomon built the City, and offered offerings: then it was that the barren bare a son. And whereas she told thee that she reared him with travail: that was the dwelling in Jerusalem. And whereas she said unto thee: my son, entering into his marriage-chamber died, and that misfortune befell her— this was the fall of Jerusalem that has come to pass. And lo! thou hast seen the pattern of her, how she mourned her son, and thou didst begin to comfort her for what had befallen. Now, the Most High seeing that thou art grieved deeply and art distressed wholeheartedly on account of her; hath shewed thee the brilliance of her glory and her majestic beauty.

This apocalyptic text has moved beyond Second Isaiah's image of Jerusalem as the barren matriarch, yet it is clearly based on that tradition. The genre is apocalyptic rather than eschatological, and the scene is allegorical rather than metaphorical. Most significantly, the climax of the passage is not the birth of children to Jerusalem but the transformation of the sorrowing woman into the beautiful city. The barrenness motif is no longer at the center of the image; the gift of the son to the barren woman is part of the history which the woman relates to Salathiel, but it is not the climax. The image of Jerusalem as mother of the Jews, anticipated in Second Isaiah and expressed in Third Isaiah, on the other hand, is cited as established tradition (Sion, the mother of us all, is in great grief, 10:8).

In his study of the vision, G. H. Box argues that the mourning mother is the heavenly Jerusalem and her son is the earthly Jerusalem. He makes a sharp distinction between the two Jerusalems because of his observation that the heavenly Jerusalem was seen as pre-existent by the original author of the vision.

> Among the realities of the eternal order is the celestial Sion, which is regarded not as something that is to come into being later, but as already in existence (see 8:52 f.). Consequently the transfiguration of the woman cannot be explained as symbolizing the glorification of the earthly Sion into the heavenly (this would imply that the heavenly Zion is not a present and eternal reality, but is yet to be), but as a revelation of the true character of the woman: the weeping mother, bewailing the loss of her son, suddenly throws off the mask

and reveals herself in her true character, and her ineffable glory. She is the eternal heavenly Zion. The 3,000 years of unfruitfulness mark the period in the world's history (from Adam to David: see vv 45-46) when no earthly counterpart of herself—a place where regular oblations could be offered to God—as yet existed. The birth of the son represents the establishment of the City and the cultus therein by David; the years of the son's life symbolize the period during which the holy City on earth was sanctified with the divine presence and the regular sacrificial worship, and the death of the son marks the fall of the city, and the cessation of sacrifice.[22]

Box's interpretation has been adopted by Jacob M. Myers in his Anchor Bible Commentary on I and II Esdras.[23] Behind both Box and Myers appears to be the work of Richard Kabisch,[24] who argues on the basis of 8:52 that the mourning woman is the heavenly Jerusalem. In this passage the phrase "the world to come has been opened" and "paradise has been opened" are parallel to the phrase "the city has been built." But the context indicates that these are prophetic perfects, which still refer to the future.[25]

But there are several problems with the interpretation which Box proposes, and all are related to a right understanding of the use of the barren matriarch and Jerusalem as mother traditions. First, Jerusalem is never portrayed as a son, nor even as masculine. The image of Jerusalem as a woman is rooted in the grammatical idiom of Semitic languages, as we have seen. Box suggests that the author has adapted the well known story of the son who dies on his wedding day (perhaps from the Book of Tobit), and that "the story was so well known to the readers that they could at once understand and see the propriety of the reference to the misfortunes of the earthly Jerusalem in the figure of the unfortunate son."[26]

But the misfortunes of the earthly Jerusalem are never portrayed in the image of a man dying on his wedding day; they are portrayed rather in the image of a mother who has lost her sons (cf. Jer 31:15, the Book of

---

[22]Ibid., 233.
[23]Cited in note 19.
[24]Richard Kabisch, *Das vierte Buch Esra* (Göttingen: Vandenhoeck und Ruprecht, 1889) 85-91.
[25]These images are illuminated by Michael Stone in his article, "Paradise in IV Ezra 4:8 and 7:36, 8:52," *JJS* 17 (1966) 85-88.
[26]Box, 239.

Lamentations, Baruch 4-5). What basis would the author's audience have for understanding Zion as a son who died on his wedding day? In Jewish literature of the Second Temple period images typically work because they are rooted in biblical tradition; it is their relation to Scriptural traditions which makes them understood and also which gives them their basis of authority.

Another problem with the interpretation which Box suggests is in his presentation of the heavenly Jerusalem as barren and mourning. In the tradition of Jerusalem as the barren and mourning woman on which the author of the vision has drawn, there is a sharp contrast between the sorrowing (destroyed) Jerusalem and the rejoicing (restored) Jerusalem. To present the heavenly Jerusalem in deep mourning is to confuse the images. In fact the image of Zion mourning over her sons is used in 10:7 precisely to portray the earthly Zion in destruction.

The argument that the mourning mother is the heavenly Zion rests on a textual emendation for which there is no evidence. In 10:45 Box translates:

> And whereas she said unto thee that she was barren thirty years: the reason is that there were three thousand years in the world before any offering was offered in (it) (i.e., the world).

The Latin of the last phrase reads: "quando non erat in ea ad huc oblatio oblata,"[27] that is, before any offering was offered *in her*, Zion. Not one version supports the reading *in eo*, yet Box adopts it. While the text indicates that 3,000 years elapsed before the Temple was built in Zion, Box emends it to say that the 3,000 years signify the period from Adam to David, before Jerusalem was established. To further support his thesis, Box emends the text in 10:46 from Solomon to David, again with no witness from the versions.[28]

The image of the heavenly Zion being barren, giving birth to the earthly Zion and then mourning his death violates all of the documented evidence of the image of Zion as the barren mother. Barrenness is a sign of the state of affairs *before* the restoration of Jerusalem. In eschatological contexts, barrenness is a reference to this side of the eschaton. To make the heavenly Zion barren is therefore in total discontinuity with the traditional significance of barrenness. It seems unlikely that the author of

---

[27] Ibid., 237.
[28] Ibid., 238.

the Ezra Apocalypse would use so many details of the tradition of Jerusalem as a barren woman in such a confusing manner. By using an established tradition the author is able to give an aura of antiquity and of authority to his work (as Second Isaiah did by reference to the Torah story). The author's use of Ezra's name as his pseudonym indicates that he sought such authority. But if the tradition is radically altered, it cannot function as authoritative; in that case the ancient authority is not invoked but challenged.

If we accept the interpretation of the mourning woman as the heavenly Zion "in disguise," then we cannot properly speak of eschatological transformation of Jerusalem. The form critical work of Claus Westermann is instructive here, for he has shown, in a study of the lament form, how the transformation of Zion functions as the resolution of a lament.

> Die Verwandlung der trauernden Frau in die erbaute Stadt zeigt die theologische Veränderung der Klage. In der Klage der Psalmen wird die Wandlung des Leides niemals zuerst bei dem Beklagten erwartet, sondern bei Gott, bei dem also, an den sich die Klage wendet. Das Entscheidende muss bei Gott geschehen, dass nämlich sein Zorn sich wendet und er sich wieder dem Klagenden zuwendet. Das ist wahrscheinlich auch im IV. Esra vorausgesetzt; aber die Wandlung wird dich faktisch an der Oberfläche des Geschehenden erwartet.[29]

The birth of the son to the barren woman therefore represents the building of the Temple in Jerusalem during the Solomonic era, and his death represents the destruction of the Temple in 70 C.E., a cruel and shattering loss.[30] The vision of the established city, the transformation of the mourning mother, indicates that the author of the work did not look for a rebuilding of Jerusalem, but rather for an apocalyptic transformation. This vision is important in the history of the Jerusalem tradition because it establishes the new idea of a heavenly Jerusalem which will replace the earthly one. Hope for the restoration of Jerusalem has turned into expectation of the descent of the heavenly Jerusalem. The historical continuity between the suffering Jerusalem and the new Jerusalem which was carefully maintained by Second and Third Isaiah and in Baruch gives way here to a radical discontinuity between the historical Jerusalem and

---

[29]Claus Westermann, "Struktur und Geschichte der Klage im Alten Testament," *ZAW* 66 (1954) 79.

[30]The work of Paul Volz (*Die Eschatologie der jüdischen Gemeinde* [Tübingen: J. C. B. Mohr, 1934]) is still very useful. See especially 376.

the heavenly city. It is not the restored city which Salathiel sees, but rather the *similitudenem ejus*, the heavenly counterpart which cannot be destroyed.

CONCLUSIONS

The three texts which we have studied in this chapter share two characteristics in common: they all present Jerusalem as the mother of the Jews, and they all arose out of the context of the destruction of Jerusalem, whether in 587 B.C.E. or in 70 C.E. The tradition of Jerusalem as mother of the Jews not in the future but in the present was developed by Third Isaiah, as we have seen. Although Third Isaiah was himself "commenting upon" or "searching" (מדרש) the words of Second Isaiah, his own words apparently met a deep need in the post-exilic community, and they soon took on a life of their own.

The image of mother Jerusalem functioned best precisely in those times when Jerusalem itself was devastated. What did it mean for the Jews to call the ruined city their mother? In all of the texts Jerusalem is either weeping for her children, who have been sent away in punishment for sin, or she is pictured as receiving them upon her breast. But in no case is mother Jerusalem herself responsible for the destruction or guilty of sin.[31] This is in contrast to the Jerusalem of Jeremiah, First Isaiah and Ezekiel, which is portrayed as a harlot and a hopelessly faithless wife.

In the image of Jerusalem as mother, the prophets and poets of the Second Temple period have separated the inhabitants of Jerusalem from the *idea* of the city itself. They have recaptured the idea of Jerusalem as mythic space, which had been manifest earlier in Israel's theology.[32]

---

[31]This dissociation of the "idea" of Jerusalem from the political realities can be seen also in the literature of Qumran. The Apostrophe to Zion (see n. 8, p. 76) is a pastiche of the prophetic images of Zion as mother. Yet the Essenes would not even enter Jerusalem because in their eyes it had been defiled by the Hasmonean high priests. Instead, they withdrew to the desert and waited (and prayed for) the day of her salvation, maintaining their identity as the true children of Zion.

[32]While it is in Third Isaiah that the spiritualization of Jerualem is most fully developed, the intimation of Jerusalem as a transcendent reality is clear in Second Isaiah and even before. The story of the development of the symbol of Zion is told brilliantly by Norman Porteous in "Jerusalem—Zion: The Growth of a Symbol," *Verbannung und Heimkehr* (ed., A. Kuschke;) (Tübingen: J. C. B. Mohr, 1961) 235-262.

While the prophets Second Isaiah and Ezekiel used the ancient mythologies in a new historical way, Third Isaiah and his successors developed the ancient myth of Jerusalem as religious idea. It represented the beginnings of the world, the presence of the deity, and the life in Eden.[33]

In the context of the destruction of Jerusalem and the despair of the people this emphasis on Jerusalem as a spiritual reality rather than as simply a city functioned as one of the sources of Jewish identity. Even with the city in ashes the reinterpretation of the ancient and well known Zion mythology made her once again the holy city, she who united all Jews. While Jeremiah and Ezekiel had attacked the doctrine of the inviolability of Zion and had portrayed the city as polluted and faithless, Third Isaiah and his successors had separated the sin of the people from the idea of Jerusalem. Jerusalem the mother who is in mourning for her sons is innocent; it is not she but her children who have sinned and are being punished. By separating the *idea* of Jerusalem from the *inhabitants* of Jerusalem through the image of a mother and her sons, the authors of this tradition have preserved the holiness of Zion. The Judahites had always understood their identity in terms of the Davidic covenant and the holy city; when the city was destroyed, a few prophets saw it as a time to change Judah's understanding of who she was (e.g., Jeremiah), while others preserved the Judahite identity by changing their understanding of the holy city and the Davidic covenant.

The renewal of the ancient Zion theology introduced after the Exile established the tradition of mother Zion, a tradition which became increasingly popular in Second Temple Judaism. While it began as a reinterpretation of an old tradition, it soon took on a life of its own, and itself became the object of expansion and reinterpretation. The image of mother Zion had responded to two important needs in post-exilic Judah: the need for a feminine religious symbol which was compatible with monotheism, and the need to understand the destruction of Jerusalem in the context of Judahite theology. The Zion tradition had proved itself adaptable; the new symbol of mother Zion would also in time prove to be surprisingly adaptable in contexts quite different from its original one.

---

[33]Frank Cross, in *Canaanite Myth and Hebrew Epic* (Cambridge: Harvard, 1973), argues that the post-exilic prophets transformed the ancient Canaanite myths of creation and conflict into eschatological images, thereby laying the foundations of apocalyptic. Paul D. Hanson in *The Dawn of Apocalyptic*, pursues Cross's thesis, especially in Zechariah 9-14. The "re-mythologizing" of Jerusalem, then, was not an isolated phenomenon, but was at the heart of post-exilic prophecy.

5
Spiritual Conception

THE IDEA OF SPIRITUAL BARRENNESS

In spite of the increasingly significant tradition of the barren women who gave birth to special sons, barrenness was a curse and a humiliation in Israel. Although the narrative told of barren women who were especially loved by YHWH, barrenness was interpreted as a sign of divine disfavor and the barren represented a class of people viewed with pity and dread. Prov 30:16 pictures Sheol as a barren womb. In Hos 9:11-14 barrenness and miscarrying wombs are to be the punishment for Ephriam's sins. Ps 107:33-34 describes Yahweh as the one who makes fruitful land barren because of the sin of its inhabitants.

Conversely, the reward for obedience is first of all fruitfulness of land, cattle and women.[1] In the ancient Near East, fruitfulness was a manifestation of divine favor; whether it came from Baal, Ishtar or Yahweh, it could not be taken for granted. For those who attributed the gift of life to Baal or Ishtar, prescribed rituals which insured its continuance were acted out. For those who attributed the gift of life to Yahweh, the original blessing of fruitfulness at creation was contingent upon Israel's faithfulness in the covenant relation.

The Deuteronomic theology, which promised that Israel's obedience would be rewarded with blessings (i.e., fruitfulness and life) and disobedience would be punished by curses (barrenness and death), intended to show that the life of the nation was dependent on Yahweh. But two things happened to this formula of blessings and curses early on in its interpretation in Israel. First, it was inevitably applied to individuals rather than to the whole nation to whom it was originally addressed. Second, it was read backwards, so that material abundance was seen as proof of righteousness

---

[1] See, e.g., Exod 23:26, Deut 7:14, Ps 107:35-38.

while personal catastrophe indicated the presence of sin. As J. A. Sanders succinctly notes:

> While Deuteronomy stressed that obedience brings blessings and disobedience brings curses, one cannot go on to assume (as many ever since Deuteronomy did assume—see the book of Job) that suffering indicates one is not elect while riches or ease on earth indicates that one is elect.[2]

This "inversion of the Deuteronomic ethic," as Sanders calls it, appears to have been widely held in Israel.[3] The speeches of Eliphaz, Bildad and Zophar in Job eloquently state the inversion, while Job steadfastly refuses to accept it. Jeremiah's ministry was a struggle against this position. In this context, the "reproach" of barrenness is not a matter of social standing; it is a sign of sin.

It is in reaction against this dominant theological position that we find, in a few isolated texts, the attempt to spiritualize the notion of fruitfulness for individuals. In a sixth century text the foreigner and the eunuch, symbols of outcasts in post-exilic Israel, become those who receive blessings greater than material prosperity and a fruitfulness better than physical fecundity:

> To the eunuchs who keep my sabbaths,
>   who choose the things that please me
>   and hold fast my covenant,
> I will give in my house and within my walls
>   a monument and a name
>   better than sons and daughters;
> I will give them an everlasting name
>   which shall not be cut off.
>   Isaiah 56:4-5

The notion that the righteous eunuch is more fertile than the disobedient father of many sons would be surprising in sixth century Israel. The prophet challenges the accepted categories of blessed and cursed, elect and outcast; precisely he who is excluded from worship turns out to be the

---

[2]"The Ethic of Election in Luke's Great Banquet Parable," *Essays in Old Testament Ethics* (ed. Crenshaw and Willis; New York: Ktav, 1974) 258.
[3]Deut 23:1 and Lev 21:17.

one who receives the blessing. The "barren" one who keeps the law is in fact the fruitful one.

But it was at Alexandria that the idea of spiritual barrenness and fruitfulness was more fully developed. Isa 56:4 is reflected upon in Wis 3:14:

> Blessed also is the eunuch whose hands have
>   done no lawless deed,
> and who has not devised wicked things against the Lord;
> for special favor will be shown him for his faithfulness,
> and a place of great delight in the temple of the Lord.

While the ancient law excluded eunuchs from the assembly of the Lord and from functioning in the Temple, Third Isaiah, followed by the author of the book of Wisdom, says that the righteous eunuch will have a place of honor in the Temple.

The context of this verse is the problem of the suffering of the righteous and the prosperity of the wicked. The position of the author is that the apparent prosperity of the wicked is an illusion, while the suffering of the innocent is temporary.

> For blessed is the barren woman who is undefiled,
> who has not entered into a sinful union;
> she will have fruit when God examines souls.
>   Wis 3:13

The righteous barren woman is not rewarded with sons, as Hannah had been, but rather with spiritual fruit.

The author uses precisely the most dreaded evils of Israelite life—barrenness and premature death—to show that misfortune and physical defects do not reflect one's standing with God; that can only be known "when God examines souls." The author's real interest is in showing that the suffering of the righteous is temporary; the promise of blessings to those who obey still obtains, but they are being stored up for the future rather than given in the present. However, this shift from the present to the future also functions to refute the view that those who are suffering must have somehow sinned.

This is a radical departure from the ancient Israelite tradition of the promise of land and descendants and of the blessings which those who lived within the covenant could expect. It was made possible by the influence of Greek philosophical concepts on Judaism. In a time of intense and widespread persecution under Antiochus Epiphanes, the problem of the suffering of the righteous took on new and urgent significance. The ability of Judaism to meet this crisis, as well as to meet the crisis of adaptation without assimilation to the Hellenistic culture, was in no small part a result of the long tradition of reinterpreting sacred traditions. Searching the Scriptures characterized Jewish life even by the time of the Book of Wisdom in the second century B.C.E. and had proved itself as a way of coping with crisis.

The restatement of the terms of the covenant in the new language of Greek philosophy reflected the indigenous strength and adaptability of the biblical traditions. The Greek dichotomy between appearance and reality, based on the Platonic concept of the εἶδη, provided a new and useful framework in which to understand the covenant promises and the present sufferings. In this framework the ancient idea that the barren woman was cursed was transformed into the notion that she who was barren now could yet, through her righteous life, bear spiritual fruit in the future which would endure beyond the children of the wicked.

PHILO AND THE "SPIRITUAL CONCEPTION" OF ISAAC

The notion of spiritual fruitfulness which is introduced in the book of Wisdom is fully developed in the writings of Philo. Philo was particularly interested in Sarah and in the story of the conception and birth of Isaac. Throughout Philo's works Isaac appears as unique among the Patriarchs. Each of the three Patriarchs represents virtue: Abraham is the virtue which is acquired by learning, and Jacob is the virtue which is acquired by practice, but Isaac is the virtue which comes by nature, without human effort.[4] This theme is carried throughout Philo's interpretations of the patriarchal narratives. Abraham and Jacob receive new names from God "because both the scholar's form of virtue and the practiser's are open to improving influences."[5] "But Isaac keeps his name, because that which is by nature rather than by diligence, goes on its way from the first equal and perfect."[6]

Similarly, Abraham and Jacob had several wives and concubines, which

---

[4] *De Somniis* i.168 (trans. F. H. Colson and G. H. Whitaker; Loeb Classical Library; Cambridge: Harvard, 1971). All quotations from Philo which follow are taken from the Loeb Edition.
[5] *De Mutatione Nominum* 88.
[6] Ibid.

represent for Philo the progression from the preliminary sciences of harmony and logic to the mastery of virtue. Isaac, however, had only one wife, because he had no need of others:

> But the self-learnt kind, of which Isaac is a member, that joy which is the best of the good emotions, is endowed with a simple nature free from mixture and alloy, and wants neither the practice nor the teaching which entails the need of the concubine as well as the legitimate forms of knowledge.[7]

Isaac has "gained the wisdom that comes without toil and trouble, because his nature is happily gifted and his soul fruitful of good."[8] Isaac alone is described consistently in Philo's writings as the one whom God has directly endowed with virtue.[9]

This description of Isaac as one with a special link to God coincides with Philo's description of the conception of Isaac by direct intervention of God to Sarah's womb:

> The Lord begat Isaac; for He is Himself Father of the perfect nature, sowing and begetting happiness in men's souls.[10]

Sarah represents ἀρετή, and Philo interprets her barrenness not as a deficiency in her, but in Abraham.

> So Sarah, the virtue which rules my soul, was a mother, but not a mother for me ... It is well then to pray that virtue may not only bear (she does that in abundance without our prayers), but also may bear for ourselves, that we, by sharing in what she sows and genders, may enjoy happiness. For in ordinary course she bears for God only, thankfully rendering the firstfruits of the blessings bestowed upon her to Him who, as Moses says, opens the womb which yet loses not its virginity (Gen 29:31)."[11]

Sarah and God have an intimate relationship, a relationship in which Sarah is fruitful. Philo goes on to say that the text does not say that Sarah did

---

[7] *De Congressu Eruditionis gratia* 36.
[8] Ibid., 37.
[9] *De Somniis* i.168 and *De Abrahamo* 52-53.
[10] *Legum Allegoria* iii.219.
[11] *De Congressu Eruditionis gratia* 6-7.

not bring forth, but that she did not bring forth *for him*, i.e., for Abraham, because he was not capable of becoming the father of the offspring of virtue without first being instructed by her handmaiden (encyclical knowledge). Abraham's union with Hagar, therefore, prepares him for his union with Sarah and his fathering of Isaac.

An interesting aspect of Philo's interpretation is his interpretation of Gen 16:2 as an example of Sarah's modesty and grace. While it is not Sarah but we who are unable to engender the works of virtue, yet she modestly calls herself barren.

> Thus she says, "The Lord has shut me out from bearing," and does not go on to add, "for you." She does not wish to seem to upbraid and reproach others for their misfortune.[12]

We see the same interpretation of Gen 16:2—the humility of Sarah in assuming the barrenness upon herself—in the rabbinic homily in *Pesikta Rabbati*.[13] The picture of Sarah in rabbinic midrashim as pious and walking in the way of virtue certainly coincides with Philo's picture of Sarah as virtue itself. In both cases Sarah has an intimate relation with God and in both cases the character of Sarah is not drawn from Genesis, but from midrashic tradition and exegetical ingenuity.

In another context, Philo again indicates that God is the father of Isaac:

> So, too the wisdom which as in motherhood brought forth the nature of the self-taught declares that God had begotten it. For when the child is born she says with pride, "The Lord has made laughter for me" (Gen 21:6). That is the same as saying "He formed, he wrought, He begot Isaac," since Isaac and laughter are the same.[14]

But the conception of Isaac is special not only beause it is from God, but also because it is for Philo a "virginal" conception; that is, Sarah became a virgin at the time of Isaac's conception. Philo interprets Gen

---

[12] Ibid., 13.

[13] See below, p. 133.

[14] *De Mutatione Nominum* 137. Cf. also *De Cherubim* 45: For he shows us Sarah conceiving at the time when God visited her in her solitude (Gen 21:1), but when she brings forth it is not to the Author of her visitation, but to him who seeks to win wisdom, whose name is Abraham.

Spiritual Conception

18:11: "It had ceased to be with Sarah after the manner of women" as evidence that God made Sarah's womb virginal at the conception of Isaac. God would not visit Sarah until the degenerate appetites which characterize women had left her; she is therefore returned to the class of pure virgins for "it is meet that God should hold converse with the truly virgin nature, that which is undefiled and free from impure touch."[15] Philo stresses that God is not the husband of a virgin, since a virgin could be defiled by passions, but rather he is the husband of the εἶδος of virginity, which is unchanging.

This interpretation of Gen 18:11 which makes Sarah a virgin at the conception of Isaac recurs several times in Philo. Her "virginity" indicates that the passions which draw us away from the pursuit of and union with God are not present in her. It represents a state of total receptivity to God:

> But among the virtues some are ever virgin, some pass from womanhood to virginity, as Sarah did: for "it ceased to be with her after the manner of women" (Gen 18:11), at the time when she first conceives Isaac, happiness personified.[16]

The woman who "was always a virgin," according to Philo, was Leah, because she was hated and "out of reach of the passions." But her alienation from men makes her close to God, from whom, Philo says, she "received the seed of wisdom, and is in birththroes, and brings forth beautiful ideas worthy of the Father who begat them."[17] Unlike Sarah, who represents virtue itself, Leah is a model of the way to virtue, for Philo exhorts his readers to imitate Leah in rejecting mortal things so that they will of necessity turn to the incorruptible God. Nevertheless, in both cases, virginity represents a state of detachment from passion and availability to God which results in "conception" by him. Philo has no hint of sexual union in his discussion of this conception; it is rather the Platonic idea of the union of the soul with the Good.

These passages all occur in the context of Philo's interest in moral and spiritual development. Philo uses the feminine imagery of becoming pregnant and becoming virgin because it expresses the relation of the soul of man to God; that is, passive, inferior and receptive. The initiative and power of God are contrasted with the dependence and weakness of the

---

[15] *De Cherubim* 42-51.
[16] *De Posteritate Caini* 134.
[17] Ibid., 135.

human soul, which waits to be empowered by union with God. In his study of male and female imagery in Philo's writings, R. A. Baer shows how the imagery of divine impregnation functions within this context of divine inspiration:

> In all of these texts, God is shown to be the source of all goodness and virtue. Man is as nothing before God. The attitude of soul required of man is one of humility, receptivity, passivity. The male-female terminology, with God as male and the human soul as female, appears to be particularly apt for expressing this kind of relationship between God and man.[18]

This is in contrast to Philo's theme of becoming male, in which man takes the initiative for disciplining himself to forsake the feminine (sense-perception) and pursue virtue.[19] Clearly Philo's imagery of divine impregnation is intended to emphasize the active and gracious role of God in his rapport with the human soul.

Interestingly, Philo uses the imagery of barrenness in the same context in which he uses virginity. We saw that Leah's status as hated made her especially receptive to God; barrenness is also interpreted as a state in which one is receptive to divine action. Speaking of Sarah as virtue, Philo says:

> For indeed virtue is barren as regards all that is bad, but shews herself a fruitful mother of the good; a motherhood which needs no midwifery, for she bears before the midwife comes.[20]

Here barrenness, like virginity, represents a state of purity and of separation fron the corruption of the senses. This parallel is drawn even more explicitly in Philo's interpretation of Isa 54:1:

> For she that is desolate, says the prophet, will have children many and fine, a saying which also is an allegory of the

---

[18]Richard A. Baer, Jr., *Philo's Use of the Categories Male and Female* (Leiden: Brill, 1970) 61.

[19]Ibid. 49-50. Philo's terminology is complex and somewhat fluid; Baer's study is very clarifying. He stresses that Philo's categories are functional rather than ontological.

[20]*De Congressu Eruditionis gratia* 3.

Spiritual Conception 99

history of the soul. For when the soul is "many," of all that is of passions and vices with her children, pleasures, desires, folly, incontinence, injustice, gathered around her, she is feeble and sick and dangerously near to death. But when she has become barren and ceases to produce these children or indeed has cast them out bodily she is transformed into a pure virgin.[21]

The new family consists of all the virtues which oppose the vices of the large family (the soul full of passions); i.e., prudence, temperance, courage, justice, etc. In the state of barrenness/pure virginity the soul is impregnated by God and brings forth virtues. The *function* of barrenness is the same as the function of virginity: it is a state of availability and receptivity which results in spiritual fruit.

Philo's allegorical interpretation in not a flight of fancy, but is based on his literal interpretation of the narratives in Genesis. In an analysis of Genesis 16 he asks "Why did not Sarah the wife of Abraham bear him children?" The literal meaning (τὸ ῥητόν) is twofold: that the son would appear more wonderful and that the conception and birth would be through the providence of God. "For when a barren woman gives birth, it is not by way of generation but the work of the divine power."[22] Whether literally in a woman or allegorically in a soul, barrenness functions as a passive and receptive object for divine initiative and grace.

Philo suggests that the idea of spiritual offspring and of fruitful virginity was the basis for the life style of certain contemporary women who live in celibacy. His description of the Therapeutae is probably influenced by his own idealism; nevertheless it indicates that the idea of spiritual fruitfulness could function as a real alternative to children. Philo describes them as women who are virgins by choice, because in their pursuit of wisdom,

> ... they have spurned the pleasures of the body and desire no mortal offspring but those immortal children which only the soul that is dear to God can bring to the birth unaided because the Father has sown in her spiritual rays (ἀκτῖνας νοητάς) enabling her to behold the verities of wisdom.[23]

---

[21] *De Praemiis et Poenis* 158-9.
[22] *Quaestiones et Solutiones in Genesin* 18.
[23] *De Vita Contemplativa* 68.

Again virginity represents for Philo a state of receptivity and of passivity which provides a place for divine activity.

SPIRITUAL CONCEPTION IN LUKE'S INFANCY NARRATIVE

In the infancy narrative of Luke the barren matriarch tradition is clearly echoed in the story of Elizabeth and Zechariah, the parents of John the Baptist. Elizabeth, like Sarah, is barren and old (Luke 1:7) and Zechariah, like Abraham, is old (Luke 1:7). We will see that in Jewish tradition Sarah and Abraham were pious and righteous people. Luke echoes this tradition in his description of Elizabeth and Zechariah as righteous before God (Luke 1:6). The tradition that Isaac was given as a result of Abraham's prayers for others may also be in the background of Luke's narrative, for it is precisely as Zechariah is sacrificing in the Temple and praying on behalf of the people that he is told he will be given a son.

Luke's infancy narrative is significant in the midrashic development of the barren matriarch tradition because it represents the first time since 1 Samuel 1 that the tradition has been used in the genre of birth narrative.[24] As a result, many of the original and most ancient functions of the traditions re-emerge in Luke's story. As in the stories in Genesis and 1 Samuel 1, the story of John's conception and birth from parents who are aged and barren marks him as a special child, with an important destiny which has been determined by God. Luke furthers this theme by the sign of Zechariah's loss of speech and the subsequent restoration of his speech at the naming of the child, and by the canticle of Zechariah in which the child's destiny is foretold (Luke 1:67-79).

But Luke's interest in the birth of John goes beyond these original functions of the barren matriarch motif, for Elizabeth's pregnancy functions primarily as an eschatological sign. Through Elizabeth and Zechariah Luke is able to express both continuity with the history of Israel and the beginning of the eschatological time. We have seen how the birth of a son to a barren woman was an eschatological sign in Jewish tradition, not only in the symbol of Jerusalem but also in the tradition of Sarah as eschatological sign. For Luke's audience the restoration of speech to the dumb

---

[24] Charles Perrot ("Les récits d'enfance dans la Haggadah," *RSR* 55 [1967] 481-518) collects some of the infancy narratives in the non-canonical literature. The emphasis is on a miraculous birth or dangers to the child's life. Barrenness, interestingly enough, is not a dominant motif.

Spiritual Conception   101

and the gift of a son to the barren would signify the beginning of the eschatological time. The annunciation to Zechariah underlines this theme by describing John in the role of Elijah, as the one who will prepare the way for the coming of Yahweh. The work of reconciliation and preparation of the people before the day of Yahweh is described in Mal 4:5-6 as the work which Elijah will be sent to do.[25]

The story of the barren and aged Elizabeth who bears a son provides a context of eschatological expectation as well as of continuity with Israel's history for the birth of Jesus. The relation between the two women prefigures the relation between John and Jesus. Elizabeth's pregnancy precedes Mary's and is a sign of the meaning of Mary's pregnancy, just as John's preaching precedes Jesus and indicates the significance of him who is coming (Luke 3:15-18).[26]

But perhaps the most important parallel which Luke draws is the parallel between Elizabeth's barrenness and Mary's virginity. The new story of the conception and birth of Jesus could be understood by means of the story of the conception and birth of John. The story of a son given to an aged and barren woman was familiar and could therefore provide an interpretive aid to the less accessible story of the virginal conception of Jesus. Since Jewish tradition provided no precedent for a virginal conception,[27] Luke used the tradition of the barren woman as a midrashic clue with which to signify the meaning of the virginal conception of Jesus.

To understand the meaning of Mary's virginity in first century Judaism, it is important to remember that virginity took on a rather specialized meaning for the church by the fourth century, and that this meaning is sometimes read back into Luke's account. As long as Christians were persecuted and put to death for their faith, the definition of Christian martyrdom was clear and the highest form of witness was the steadfast affirmation of one's faith even to the point of death at the hands of a tormentor. When Christians were no longer persecuted, death was replaced by virginity as the new form of Christian martyrdom. This espousal of virginity as a positive value was the result of complex factors and influences which we cannot study here. But the result was that quite early

---

[25] For further discussion of this theme see R. E. Brown, *The Birth of the Messiah* (New York: Doubleday, 1977) 375-392.

[26] Ibid., 250-253, on the ways in which the structure of the infancy narratives show this.

[27] The evidence is reviewed in Brown, *Birth*, 521-524.

Mary is represented as virginal by choice and as the model for the celibate Christian life.[28] In ancient Israelite and early Jewish thinking, however, virginity had no such significance or positive value. It was in giving birth to sons that a woman fulfilled the destiny for which she was created and her obligation to her husband. Virgins were protected because of their prospective value as wives and mothers; maternity, not virginity, was the highest vocation for women.

In Luke's infancy narrative, both barrenness and virginity are "low estates" which are elevated by God. Just as God took away the ὀνειδός of Elizabeth (Luke 1:25, echoing Gen 30:23), so also he regarded the ταπείνωσις of Mary. Because the Magnificat of Mary is modelled on the Song of Hannah, Luke clearly intended to evoke the story of Hannah as background for the story of Mary.[29] Luke 1:48, ὅτι ἐπέβλεψεν ἐπὶ τὴν ταπείνωσιν τῆς δούλης αὐτοῦ is based on Hannah's prayer in 1 Sam 1:11: ἐὰν ἐπιβλέπων ἐπιβλέψῃς ἐπὶ τὴν ταπείνωσιν τῆς δούλης σου. The ταπείνωσιν τῆς δουλης recalls the ταπείνωσιν τῆς δούλης of Hannah. Like Hannah, Mary symbolized the *anawim*, the poor who are exalted by Yahweh. Both the barren woman and the virgin are ταπειναί and both are δοῦλαι.

The fructifying of the barren woman as the sign of the vindication of the humiliated was well known by the first century C.E., as we have seen. It originated in the story of Hannah, which reinterpreted the story of the barren mothers into a sign of Yahweh's vindication of Israel before her enemies. In Jewish tradition this motif of vindication became elaborated and was read back into the stories of Sarah and of Samson's mother as well. Sarah particularly was the "low tree which was exalted." And of course the motif of humiliation and exaltation was elaborated most extensively in the traditions of Zion as the barren woman who was made the joyful mother of sons.

For Luke, the exaltation of the woman of low estate fuctions in two

---

[28] *Birth*, 304. See also Eleanor McLaughlin, "Sex and Anti-sex in the Church Fathers," *Male and Female* (ed., Urban Holmes; New York: Seabury, 1976), and "Misogynism and Virginal Feminism in the Fathers of the Church," by Rosemary Ruether, in *Religion and Sexism* (New York: Simon and Schuster, 1974).

[29] Though we note that Brown sees also a historical reminiscence of Mary behind the image of her as one who hears the word and does it (*Birth*, 316-319).

ways. First, it reflects his theology of the *anawim* as the people of God.[30] In Luke's Gospel it is the poor, the downtrodden and the women who recognize Jesus and who symbolize the reversal of human values which characterized the kingdom of God. Second, the way in which God creates life out of Mary's virginal womb prefigures the Resurrection. Several studies of the virginal conception have demonstrated the relation between Luke's account of the virginal conception and the early Christian formula about the Resurrection in Rom 1:3-4.[31] The words of Gabriel to Mary in Luke 1:35:

> The Holy Spirit will come upon you
> and the power of the Most High will overshadow you;
> therefore the child to be born will be called holy,
> the Son of God.

use the same language as the formula in Rom 1:3-4:

> ... the gospel concerning his Son, who was descended from David according to the flesh and designated Son of God in power according to the Spirit of holiness by his resurrection from the dead. ...

In both texts the context is the same: that Jesus is both of the house of David and also Son of God. Both texts name the Holy Spirit as the agent by which Jesus was the Son of God, only in Romans it happens at the Resurrection while in Luke it occurs at the conception.[32] In a study of the function of virginal conception in early Christian theology, L. Legrande has demonstrated how the conception of Jesus by the Holy Spirit was based on the early Christian tradition of the Holy Spirit as life-giver. Just as in Ezek 37:1-11 the Spirit vivified the dry bones of Israel into a new people, so it was by the power of the Holy Spirit that Jesus was raised from the dead. Just as the Holy Spirit brought life out of death in the Resurrection, so also the Spirit gave life out of the lifelessness of Mary's virginity.

---

[30] The canticles especially show Luke's interest in the *anawim* (*Birth*, 350-355).

[31] L. Legrande, M. E. P., "Fécondité virginalale selon Esprit dans le Nouveau Testament," *NRT* 84 (1962) 785-805; *Birth*, 29-31 and 311-316.

[32] For Brown this reflects the "backward development of Christology." See *Birth*, 26-32.

> Dans la theologie de l'evangile de l'enfance, et meme si Luc ne fut pas conscient de l'analogie, la virginite de Marie joue le role de la Croix dans la theologie paulinienne. La ταπεινωσις de la Vierge prend tout son sens dans sa similitude avec l'εταπεινωσεν du Calvaire (Phil 2, 8). Elle n'est pas bonne en se meme car, d'elle-meme, elle n'est qu'abaissement, humiliation. Comme la mort du Christ ne serait rien sans la Resurrection, la virginite de Marie, pour l'evangeliste, n'aboutirait a rien et ne serait que misere sans l'intervention vivifiante de Espirit.[33]

Like the barrenness of Sarah, Hannah and Jerusalem, Mary's virginity represented weakness which Yahweh transformed into power, and death which he changed into life.

The association of the themes of Resurrection and conception is made through the idea of the power of the Holy Spirit, reflecting the early Christian belief that it was through the Holy Spirit that Jesus was empowered as the Son of God. This association between the divine power to give life in the face of death and the divine gift of conception had already been made in the Song of Hannah:

κύριος θανατοῖ καὶ ζωογονεῖ, κατάγει εἰς ᾅδου καὶ ἀνάγει

> The Lord kills and brings to life
> He brings down to Sheol and raises up.
>
> 1 Sam 2:6

For anyone searching the Scriptures to answer questions about Jesus, the verbs ζωογονεῖ and ἀνάγει fairly leap out of the text. Precisely this image of Sheol giving up its prey before the power of Yahweh is used by Luke in Peter's address in Acts 2. In describing the Resurrection Luke has Peter say: ὃν ὁ θεὸς ἀνέστησεν λύσας τὰς ὠδῖνας τοῦ θανάτου, καθότι οὐκ ἦν δυνατὸν κρατεῖσθαι αὐτὸν ὑπ' αὐτοῦ.

> But God raised him up, having loosed the pangs of death because it was not possible for him to be held by it.
>
> Acts 2:24

Further, in 1 Sam 2:8 Hannah's song continues the image of raising up the

---

[33]"Fécondité virginale," 793.

humbled: ἀνιστᾷ ἀπὸ γῆς πένητα καί ἀπὸ κοπρίας ἐγείρει πτωχόν. The verbs ἀνιστᾷ and ἐγείρει were used by Christians to describe the Resurrection (ἀνιστᾷ is used by Luke in Acts 3:15, 4:10, 5:30, 10:40, 13:30, 37, 26:8. ἐγείρει is used by Luke in Acts 2:24, 32, 3:26, 13:33-34, 17:31). In the Song of Hannah the motifs of conception by a barren woman, power over death and exaltation of the *anawim* are all woven together. Luke's infancy narrative centers around precisely these themes: the conception of Jesus by the Holy Spirit prefigures the Resurrection by the Holy Spirit, and the Resurrection initiates the reign of God, a time when the *anawim* are exalted. By reflecting on the Scriptures in the context of early Christian preaching about the Resurrection, Luke found the basis for his infancy narrative. For Luke the meaning of the virginal conception of Jesus was prefigured in the conception of Samuel to the barren Hannah.

But an important question remains unanswered. How can the physical conception which Hannah experienced parallel the spiritual conception which Luke describes in his infancy narrative? Is there any precedent in Jewish tradition for associating barrenness with virginity and physical conception with spiritual conception? Is there a missing link in the midrashic development of the barren matriarch story which can explain the surprising way in which Luke used it?

Luke used the barren matriarch traditions as references of authority, to ground his proclamation of who Jesus was solidly in the Scriptures. But how would Luke's audience have understood the relation between the aged and barren Elizabeth and the young virgin Mary? Is there a midrashic use of the barren matriarch tradition prior to Luke's which would have provided a context in which Luke's story was understood?

The association between the barren woman and the virgin and between physical conception and spiritual conception occurs in the tradition of Jerusalem as mother of Israel. We have seen in our study of the Jerusalem traditions that the city was personified simultaneously as בתולת ישראל and as עקרה. It was Second Isaiah who first made this association explicit, and it has continued and elaborated, as we have seen, in the apocalyptic literature as well as in the synagogue lectionaries and homilies.[34] Paul's use of the midrashic traditions about Sarah and Jerusalem, as we shall see, demonstrates that the association was known and used in the earliest Christian thinking.

---

[34]Evidence of a link between Sarah and Jerusalem in the liturgical traditions of early Judaism is found in Gal 4:21-31 as well as in rabbinic midrashim, as we will show in the next chapter.

It is significant that Luke evokes the figure of Sarah, for it is Sarah, of all the matriarchs, who is most closely identified with Jerusalem. Luke does not simply recall Sarah in the aged and barren figure of Elizabeth; he links Sarah to Mary herself. When Mary responds to Gabriel's news with the question "How can this be?", Gabriel answers her in the same words with which God answered Sarah's laughter of disbelief at his news to her:

LXX Gen 18:14

$$\mu\grave{\eta} \ \mathrm{\mathring{a}\delta υνατε\tilde{\iota} \ παρ\grave{α} \ τ\tilde{\wp} \ θε\tilde{\wp} \ \mathring{ρ}\tilde{η}μα;}$$

Luke 1:37

$$\mathrm{\mathring{o}τι \ οὐκ \ ἀδυνατήσει \ παρ\grave{α} \ το\tilde{υ} \ θεο\tilde{υ} \ π\tilde{α}ν \ \mathring{ρ}\tilde{η}μα.}$$

The important point about the virginal conception is not that it is an altogether new and superior form of miraculous birth story, but, on the contrary, that it so richly brings together all the traditions developed around the barren matriarchs and Jerusalem as mother. The story of the virginal conception cannot be understood apart from the matrix of traditions which linked Sarah, Jerusalem and the eschatological community.[35]

It is not necessary to argue that Mary is presented as a "type" of Jerusalem, or the Daughter Zion. The supposed linguistic parallels between Luke 1:28-31 and Zeph 3:14-17 are simply not convincing enough to demonstrate that Luke consciously patterned his annunciation to Mary on Zephaniah's annunciation to Jerusalem. Luke is not saying that Mary *is* the Daughter Zion.[36] Rather he is presenting Mary's story in the context of

---

[35]While Reginald Fuller, in his review of Brown's *Birth*, *CBQ* 40 (1978) 116-120, is on the right track, it is far too schematic to say that the virginal conception originated from Jewish reflection on the birth of Isaac. There is a whole complex of midrashic traditions, of which the birth of Isaac is only one, behind Luke's presentation of the virginal conception.

[36]This position has become so popular as to be automatically repeated, uncritically, in almost every treatment of Mary, save that of Brown in *Birth*, 319-329. These include Max Thurian, *Mary, Mother of All Christians* (New York: Herder and Herder, 1964); Lucien Deiss, *Mary, Daughter of Zion* (Collegeville, MN: Liturgical, 1972); John McHugh, *The Mother of Jesus in the New Testament* (London: Barton, Longman & Todd, 1974); and Andrew Greeley, *The Mary Myth* (New York: Seabury, 1977).

the barren matriarch traditions, which include the Daughter Zion, because for him that complex of traditions is the hermeneutical key to understanding the virginal conception of Jesus. It is the figure of Jerusalem as mother, then, which provides the link between Sarah's barrenness and Mary's virginity. But Luke was not the first to use the Sarah-Jerusalem tradition in the genre of the nascent Christian Gospel.[37] Let us turn now to the earliest use of these traditions in the NT.

SARAH AND JERUSALEM IN GAL 4:21-31

In Gal 4:21-31 Paul answers a question in the Galatian community about the status of the Law with a midrash on the identity of Israel. The passage has three sections, each of which centers on a passage from Scripture:

4:22-23 centers on Gen 16
4:24-27 centers on Isa 54:1
4:28-31 centers on Gen 21:9-10

The issue in the Galatian community was about the status of the Law; the community was divided over the question of whether circumcision and observing the laws of Kashrut were necessary to their new faith in Jesus. It is a question of *ethos*, of how to live out their vocation which has confounded the Galatians. But Paul responds to their problem of *ethos* in the language of *muthos*;[38] for him the problem of how they should live was rooted in their concept of who they were.

However, Fuller, in the review of Brown cited in Note 35, makes a point worth quoting here. Of Brown's rejection of this Daughter Zion parallel to Mary, Fuller says: "Brown is right so far as the intention of Luke is concerned. But, as J. A. Sanders has persuasively argued, texts have a life of their own, and when taken into the canon acquire new possibilities of meaning when related to other texts."

[37] The motifs of barrenness and virginity were already linked by Philo, as we have seen, but on a metaphysical rather than a midrashic basis. While we can say that Philo was part of the Lucan milieu, it is impossible to show any dependence of Luke on Philo at this point. The dependence of Luke on the midrashic development of the barren matriarch traditions, on the other hand, is clear.

[38] The terminology is from Sanders, "Adaptable for Life: The Nature and Function of Canon," in *Magnalia Dei, The Mighty Acts of God. Essays on the Bible and Archeology in Memory of G. Ernest Wright.* Eds., F. M. Cross, W. E. Lemke and P. D. Miller; Garden City: Doubleday, 1976.

Paul argued in the third chapter of Galatians that it was not the Law which gave identity to the sons of Abraham but the promise. The Law, coming four hundred and thirty years after the promise, functioned as a babysitter until the promise was fulfilled by Christ.[39] For Paul the true descendants of Abraham are those who share in the promise (Rom 4:11, 16; 9:6-9); it is they who are entitled to call Abraham "our father" (Rom 4:1, 12, 16). For Paul, the promise of Gen 21:12 that "through Isaac shall your descendants be named" is fulfilled in Christ. But what is the relationship between the birth of Isaac and the identity of the Christian community?

In earliest Christian thought the story of Jesus was interpreted, at least in part, by reference to the story of Isaac. By the first century C.E., the Akedah, the story of the binding of Isaac, had become central in Jewish speculation about the relationship between God and Israel.[40] There is strong evidence that the Akedah was widely interpreted as having redemptive value for Israel; Abraham's willingness to sacrifice Isaac had the same effect as an actual sacrifice. The Akedah was interpreted by the principle of "measure for measure"; because Abraham had listened to God's request to sacrifice his son, now God would listen to Israel's requests (in prayer) for deliverance from distress.[41] Nils Dahl has proposed that in early Christian theology the principle of measure for measure was followed "to its bitter end, saying that as Abraham offered up his son, so God offered up His own son for Isaac's children."[42] The image of Jesus in the Passion Narrative also echoes the Akedah: like Isaac he carries the wood, like Isaac in Jewish tradition he goes willingly to fulfill his father's will, and like the Akedah, the Passion is described as a test (cf. the verb ἐπείραξεν in the LXX of Gen 22:1 and in the words to the disciples in Gethsemane, Matt 26:41; Mark 14:38; Luke 22:28, 40, 46; the noun πειρασμός is used).

But there is evidence that Isaac also had another significance for Paul. Not only his "sacrifice" but also his conception was used to interpret the

---

[39]The translation is Krister Stendahl's (oral tradition).

[40]See the studies of Nils Dahl, "The Atonement—An Adequate Reward for the Akedah?" in *The Crucified Messiah* (Minneapolis: Augsburg, 1974) 146-160, of Robert J. Daly, "The Soteriological Significance of the Sacrifice of Isaac," *CBQ* 39 (1977) 45-75, and of Geza Vermes, "Redemption and Genesis xxii—The Binding of Isaac and the Sacrifice of Jesus," in *Scripture and Tradition in Judaism* (Leiden: Brill, 1961) 193-227.

[41]"The Atonement," 153.

[42]Ibid.

life of Jesus. For Paul the way in which the promise was begun foreshadowed the way in which it was to be fulfilled, and he appears to draw a parallel between the conception of Isaac and the Resurrection of Jesus. In Rom 4:16-17 Paul draws an analogy between Abraham's faith that God would give him a son and the Christian's faith that God raised Jesus from the dead. Isaac was conceived not according to the flesh but according to the Spirit (Gal 4:2), just as Jesus was raised by the Spirit.

The "spiritual conception" of Isaac functions at the heart of Paul's argument that the Christians are the true sons of Abraham and heirs of the promise. In Rom 4:16-17 Paul links the God who made Abraham the father of many nations with the God who gives life to the dead. The word "dead" is Paul's key between the conception of Isaac and the Resurrection of Jesus. So important to Paul is this link that he makes the point twice, first by interpreting Gen 17:5 and immediately following, by interpreting Gen 15:6. In Rom 4:17 Paul interprets the promise to Abraham in Gen 17:5 as being fulfilled "in the presence of the God in whom he believed, who gives life to the dead and calls into existence things that do not exist." The God who made Abraham the father of many nations (and of "us all," as Paul says in Rom 4:16), is the God who gives life to the dead. For Paul's community the phrase "gives life to the dead" can have only one meaning. The life which is given to Abraham in the birth of Isaac is therefore associated with the life which was given to Jesus in the Resurrection.

Paul makes the same point with more clarity in the next verse. The promise given to Abraham in Gen 15:5 (and the response of Abraham in Gen 15:6) is also interpreted by the key word "dead." Paul says:

> He did not weaken in faith when he considered his own body, which was as good as dead because he was about a hundred years old, or when he considered the barrenness of Sarah's womb.

Abraham's old age and Sarah's barrenness are like death, which Abraham believed could be made alive by God. Paul concludes the argument with an explicit reference to the Resurrection:

> That is why his faith was "reckoned" to him as righteousness (Gen 15:6). But the words, "it was reckoned to him" were written not for his sake alone, but for ours also. It will be reckoned to us who believe in him that raised from the dead Jesus our Lord, who was put to death for our trespasses and raised for our justification.

God's role in the conception of Isaac is parallel to his role in the Resurrection of Jesus. The barrenness of Sarah is for Paul a pre-figuring of the death of Jesus; in both cases God brought life out of death. If God's role in the two events is parallel, even more important for Paul in this passage is the response of Abraham. Just as his faith that God could bring life out of death was the basis for his justification, so also the Christians' faith that God brought life out of death is their justification. The promise was fulfilled in the same way it began: by the power of God which brought life out of death. Begun in the conception of Isaac, it was fulfilled in the Resurrection of Jesus.

But the problem before us is Paul's use of Sarah and Jerusalem in Gal 4:21-31; we have examined the only other mention of Sarah's barrenness in the Pauline corpus in order to illuminate the allegory of Sarah and Hagar. The parallel which Paul draws between the barrenness of Sarah and the death of Jesus and between the conception of Isaac and the Resurrection of Jesus is presupposed in his midrash in Gal 4:21-31.

In the first section of his midrash, Paul distinguishes between the sons of Hagar and the sons of Sarah by using the dichotomy of flesh/promise and slave/free. The sharp distinction between Sarah as free and Hagar as slave was developed in Jewish tradition. It is impossible to prove that this development occurred prior to the first century C.E., but the presence of "anti-Hagar" material in the Palestinian Targums suggests that its origins are early.[43] In this tradition Hagar was given to Sarah and Abraham as part of the bounty they received from Pharaoh after the incident related in Gen 12:10-20.

But the distinction between slave and free is interpreted by Paul in the distinction between flesh and promise. Ishmael was conceived by the union of Abraham and Hagar, but Isaac was conceived by the intervention of Yahweh. It was, as the Targum Pseudo-Jonathan said, a miracle.[44] We have seen in our study of Romans 4 that the conception of Isaac was extraordinary in Paul's view. The early Jewish tradition which heightened the miracle of Isaac's conception and birth is echoed in Paul's

---

[43]See my article "The Mistress and the Maid: Midrashic Traditions Behind Gal: 4:21-31," *The Bible and Liberation* (ed., Norman K. Gottwald and Antoinette C. Wire; Berkeley: Community for Religious Research and Education, 1976) 94-101. For the significance of the Palestinian Targums, in which the reference to Hagar occurs, see Roger le Déaut, *Introduction à la Littérature Targumique* (Rome: Biblique Pontifical, 1966).

[44]See the citation on page 124.

Spiritual Conception 111

description of what God did for Sarah according to the promise and by the spirit. But it had a different meaning for Paul. For Paul the "spiritual conception" of Isaac meant that those who shared in the power of the spirit which had engendered Isaac were the true sons of Sarah and Abraham and heirs to the promise.

In the second part of his midrash Paul moves from the image of Sarah as the mother of the Christians to the image of Jerusalem as the mother of the Christians. He uses the form of allegory to make Hagar the mother of the past and Sarah the mother of the future,[45] but the argument depends on the unstated relation between Sarah and Jerusalem. Why does Paul give the citation from Isa 54:1 and confuse the contrast between Sarah and Hagar with the contrast between the present Jerusalem and the Jerusalem which is above?

The relation between Genesis 16 and Isaiah 54 reflects liturgical as well as midrashic tradition. In the lectionary lists found in the Cairo Geniza and studied by J. Mann,[46] the Haftara to Genesis 16 is Isa 54:1-9. The lectionary is based on the triennial cycle of the Palestinian synagogues, which was in use in the first century C.E. It was replaced by the annual cycle used in the synagogues of Babylonia, according to Mann, because of the hegemony of the Babylonian Gaonate over diaspora Judaism. However, a considerable body of midrashic material, incorporated in the homilies on the lectionary readings, had become associated with readings of the triennial cycle, and this material was often preserved in rabbinic traditions and homilies long after the triennial cycle had been abandoned. We will see that the rabbinic interpreters associated the seven barren mothers, with Sarah as the first and Jerusalem as the last. While many of these traditions occur in texts edited in the eighth, ninth or tenth centuries C.E., the association which Paul makes between Genesis 16 and Isa 54:1 is evidence that these texts were related at least by the first century C.E. Paul cites and uses Palestinian midrashic traditions;[47] it is likely that his association of the barren Sarah and the barren Jerusalem is

---

[45]On the allegory see H. Schiler, *Der Brief an die Galater* (Göttingen: Vandenhoeck und Ruprecht, 1965), and Wilhelm Koepp, "Die Abraham-Midraschimkette des Galater-briefs als das vorpaulinische heidenchristliche Urtheologumenon," *Wissenschaftliche Zeitschrift der Universitat Rostock*, 2. Jahrgang, Heft 3. 181-187.
[46]*The Bible as Read and Preached in the Old Synagogue* (Cincinnati, 1940).
[47]See the study of P. Grelot, "La naissance d'Isaac et celle de Jésus," *NRT* 94 (1972) 463-77, especially 472-75.

also a Palestinian tradition, which he knew from the lectionary cycle of the synagogue.

But if Paul's association between Sarah, our mother, and Jerusalem, our mother, is based on liturgical tradition, it is not limited to that tradition. We have seen that in Baruch and 4 Ezra Jerusalem is called "the mother of us all"; this image of Jerusalem as mother is picked up from the sectarian literature and incorporated into the literature of rabbinic Judaism, though it is impossible to say when this happened. However, Jerusalem, "our mother," in both sectarian and rabbinic literature is described as being in mourning, devastated or awaiting the birth of her sons.[48] The image of Jerusalem as the mother in mourning for her children is based on Jeremiah's description of Rachel weeping for her children in Jer 31:15. But the image of Jerusalem giving birth to sons, whether it signifies the restoration of Jerusalem in history or the beginning of the world to come, is based on Sarah, who gave birth when it seemed to be impossible.

In naming the Jerusalem which is above as our mother, Paul departs from the tradition. It is not the Jerusalem in mourning which is mother to the Christians, but the heavenly Jerusalem. Unlike the Jews who called Jerusalem "our mother," Paul was not waiting for Jerusalem to give birth to sons. For Paul, the prophecy of Isaiah had already been fulfilled in the birth of the Christian community. The Galatians were not the "natural" sons of Jerusalem; they were rather the sons whom the prophet had promised and who signalled the new age. Pre-figured in the birth of Isaac, foretold in the prophecy of Isaiah, the fulfillment of the prophecy had come in the Resurrection and the Galatian Christians were sons of the new age. That they did not understand their identity as the true heirs of the promise, those who lived in the time of fulfillment, was a source of pain to Paul.

How has the context in which Paul interpreted the barren matriarch tradition affected his use of the tradition? His methods and his material are traditional, yet his results are new. We have seen that Paul has drawn on the story of Sarah not in its biblical form, but in its interpreted form in early Judaism. The relation between Sarah and Jerusalem, the image of Jerusalem as mother of a people, and the idea of spiritual conception over against physical conception all reflect early Jewish interpretations of the barren matriarch stories, and all function for Paul. Moreover, Paul appears to have incorporated an early Christian tradition which saw in Isaac a figure like Jesus. Although the *ways* in which the Isaac typology

---

[48]See the references and discussion in "The Mistress and the Maid."

Spiritual Conception 113

functioned in earliest Christianity are not entirely clear, as our evidence is fragmentary and the Isaac-Jesus relation was not pursued in Christian tradition, that the story of Isaac did function to help make sense out of the story of Jesus is clear.

But Paul has not only drawn on midrashic traditions surrounding the barren mothers, he has also used them in ways which were traditional. For Paul the relation between Sarah and Jerusalem functions as a paradigm for God's activity: what he did for Sarah in the past is what he will do for Jerusalem in the future. It was in this context that the relation between Sarah and Jerusalem originated with Second Isaiah, and continued to function in Jewish tradition, both before and after Paul. For Paul the image of Jerusalem as mother functions to unify his community and to give identity to his people. Again, it was precisely in this context that the image originated in Third Isaiah and continued to function in the literature of early Judaism. The image of spiritual conception is complex in its functions, as we have seen, and Paul's use of it reflects this complexity. Paul seems to have particularly adopted the function of the spiritual fructifying of barrenness as a sign of God's power to use that which is disregarded by men and to raise up that which is humiliated.

What then is the difference between Paul's use of the traditions and the early Jewish use? For Paul, all Scripture is interpreted in the context of the Passion and Resurrection of Jesus. The difference, for Paul, is one of timing. That which was pre-figured in Sarah and promised to Jerusalem has been given. The action of God in Jesus functioned for Paul as a kind of hermeneutical principle, a context in which all of Scripture was to be understood. That is why the tradition of spiritual conception is used to interpret the identity of physical "children"; the Scriptures have been actualized for Paul and apply to the present.

THE RELATION BETWEEN PAUL'S SARAH AND LUKE'S MARY

By interpreting the Resurrection and the new life in the spirit in the context of the patriarchal birth narratives and their midrashic developments, Paul provided the basis for an infancy narrative of Jesus. The important question for Luke is not how the birth of Jesus came about, but the meaning of his birth. Behind Luke's narrative is proclamation, a proclamation very similar to that of Paul.[49] But the categories of proclamation and birth story were already united in Paul; the themes of conception and birth functioned for Paul as part of his proclamation. Luke has used the Pauline formula, and by combining it with the scanty information from earliest Christian tradition about the origins of Jesus, has given the relation between barrenness, virginity and the power of God a life of its own.[50]

---

[49] The proclamation of the infancy narrative, in fact, foreshadows the proclamation of Luke's gospel as a whole (so Brown).

[50] Luke develops the figure of Mary as the mother of the church, as does John. See "Fécundité virginal" 800-805, and Brown, *The Gospel According to John* (Garden City: Doubleday, 1966) 107-111. The symbolism is developed along different lines in Revelation 21.

6
The Mothers and the Rabbis

In the post-exilic prophetic literature the Pentateuchal tradition of the barren matriarchs was joined to the prophetic tradition of Jerusalem as the desolate wife. The limit of this tradition can be seen in Third Isaiah, who combined the ancient Jebusite mythology about Jerusalem as omphalos and residence of the Magna Mater with Second Isaiah's image of Jerusalem, the barren woman. From this complex of traditions Mother Zion emerged to become a standard part of the eschatological imagery of the Second Temple period.

The rabbinic midrashim are not part of this development, but represent a very different school within Judaism. In the interpretations which the rabbis give to the stories of the barren matriarchs we are privileged to catch a glimpse of some of the popular piety of early Judaism. If the two functions of Scripture in Second Temple Judaism were to answer questions of identity and life style,[1] to instruct Israel in who she was and how she could live out her vocation, the rabbinic midrashim tended to focus on the latter, while the prophetic and eschatological literature emphasized the former.

The rabbinic midrashim do not present a unified and standard interpretation of the barren matriarchs; rather, the literature is characterized by a rich diversity of interpretations. The different interpretations arose out of different homiletical needs; because the texts were treated in many

---

[1]The phrase is from J. A. Sanders, "Adaptable for Life: The Nature and Function of Canon," in *Magnalia Dei*, 531-60. On the relation between these two foci in early Scripture interpretation, see J. A. Sanders, "Torah," in the *IDBSup* (Nashville: Abingdon, 1976) 909-911, and "Torah and Paul" in *God's Christ and His People* (Nils Dahl Festschrift; ed., Wayne Meeks; Oslo: Universitetsforlaget, 1977) 132-140.

different contexts they fulfilled different functions. Most of the important texts are part of homiletical midrashim, sermons written for the synagogue liturgy, in which the biblical text was interpreted in the context of all of the lections for the day. The reading from Torah, Prophets and Writings together set the theme of the day, and while the homily might range far from the theme, it would always engage the three lections and relate them to a common theme. We will classify the midrashim, then, according to the *motifs* with which the barren women are associated in order to discern the function of the tradition in rabbinic preaching.[2]

---

[2]A methodological note is in order here. I began by checking the Targums, reading the pertinent passages in Genesis, Judges 13, 1 Samuel 1 and Isa 54:1. Next I read through those parashot in *Gen. Rab.* which commented on the pertinent passages in Genesis. This allowed me to read the materials in context and to begin by trying to listen to the rabbis rather than simply looking for answers to my questions. Next I turned to A. Hyman's concordance to the rabbinic literature, again checking the listings for the pertinent narrative and prophetic passages. This allowed me to have some control of the vast corpus of rabbinic literatue. By pursuing the references given by Hyman, I began to see the many different contexts in which the barren matriarch tradition occurred, and later began to see certain patterns emerging which helped make sense out of these different contexts.

Next I checked the works of Pseudo-Philo and Josephus, particularly the re-telling of the biblical stories. These are important sources because they can be dated with more accuracy than the rabbinic sources.

I then turned to Strack and Billerback's *Kommentar zum Neuen Testament aus Talmud u. Midrasch* (München, 1922-28), reading through the references given at Matthew 1 and Luke 1-2, to see whether I could pick up anything I had missed from Hyman. Finally I checked the collection which was my introduction to the midrashic literature, ספר האגדה (ed., Bialik and Ravnitzky; Tel Aviv: Dvir). While this collection did not turn up anything new, I did gain a respect for it, as so many of the traditions which I had culled form the rabbinic sources were represented. As an intermediate step to help students move from the Tanak to the unpointed rabbinic texts, it is still useful.

The problem of method, aside from the vastness of the literature and the paucity of indices to it, is that the work requires two separate tasks. One must somehow try to get a bird's eye view of the rabbinic literature to have before one the range of traditions developed on a given motif or passage. It is equally important not to simply catalog those traditions but to try to understand how they functioned in their contexts and what they meant to the people who heard them. Hence, one cannot simply read

How were the old stories of barren women able to help answer the contemporary questions of how in this time and in this place Jews could live out their vocation of sanctifying the Name? The remarkable creativity of the rabbis and the opportunities which preaching posed for interpreting the ancient texts anew resulted in a rich tradition of the barren matriarchs as beloved figures in popular piety.

THE MOTIF OF THE SEVEN BARREN WOMEN

One of the favorite rabbinic methods of interpretation is the practice of collecting biblical texts which have some similarity and interpreting the whole as a group, using the same hermeneutical principle on all of the texts. This practice stems from the fundamental principle of midrashic interpretation which arose as early as the Targums: The Bible is interpreted by the Bible. That is, a biblical passage is best understood when it is interpreted by means of another biblical passage. The formalized rabbinic hermeneutical rules, such as *Gezerah Shawah* (inference by analogy) are a result of applying this broad hermeneutical principle in very concrete ways.

It is not surprising that the rabbis associated the stories of the barren women with each other; we have seen that this association began very early. In the midrash, however, this association follows an established literary pattern, which provides the basis for interpretation. The form of the "enumeration of scriptural examples," studied extensively by W. Sibley Towner, is one of the most important form critical studies of rabbinic midrashim.[3] I will follow Towner's classifications wherever possible.

Bereshith Aggadah

'*Ag.Ber.* is based on the triennial lectionary and consists of homilies on Genesis, divided into three sections: the reading from Genesis, the haftarah from the prophets, and a reading from the Psalms. This midrash is

---

horizontally across all of the rabbinic literature, as a concordance encourages, but one must also read vertically, trying to see how a given tradition fits into the work in which it is preserved. Often the liturgical context in which the midrash was used gave another dimension of meaning which would be missed if one read the midrash in isolation.

[3]Wayne Sibley Towner, *The Rabbinic "Enumeration of Scriptural Examples"* (Leiden: Brill, 1973).

from the haftarah, 1 Sam 1:11, to the Seder Gen 30:22 (And God remembered Rachel).[4]

> And she vowed a vow and said "If thou wilt indeed look." I am barren and Zion is barren, as it is written, "Sing, O barren one" (Isa 54:1). If you will look upon me you will surely look upon Zion, and remember me, and not forget your maidservant, (the same will apply) to Zion. There are seven barren women, corresponding to the seven days of creation. The first is Sarah, of whom the saying, "Now Sarah was barren" (Gen 11:30) corresponds to the first day. What was created on the first day? The heavens and the earth. The owner of this who created it is the Holy One, blessed be He, as it is written: "Blessed be Abram by El Elyon, maker of heaven and earth" (Gen 14:19). The second is Rebecca, as it is written, "And Isaac prayed to the Lord for his wife, because she was barren (ibid. 25:21). This corresponds to the second day. What was created on the second day? "Let there be a firmament in the midst of the heavens. And let it divide the waters from the waters" (ibid. 1:6). Rachel also gave birth to two: Jacob and Esau, as it is written, "I have separated you from the peoples" (Lev 20:24). The third is Leah, as it is written, "When the Lord saw that Leah was hated, he opened her womb" (Gen 29:31). This corresponds to the third day, of which it is said "The earth brought vegetation" (ibid. 1:12). "Now Reuben went out in the days of the wheat harvest" (Gen 30:14). The fourth is Rachel, corresponding to the fourth day of creation. What was created on it? The sun, the moon, the stars and the planets, as it is written, "And God said, 'Let there be lights'" (Gen 1:14). Now Joseph the son of Rachel stood, and they bowed down to him, as it is written, "Behold, the sun, the moon and eleven stars were bowing down to me" (ibid. 37:9). The fifth is Hannah, corresponding to the fifth day. What was created on it? "Let birds fly above the earth" (Gen 1:20). This was Samuel the son of Hannah, for just as a bird can fly from place to place and from province to province, and at the end return to its nest, so was Samuel occupied with the affairs of Israel, and was going to all the places, as it is written, "And he went on a circuit year by year . . ." and "Then he would come back to Ramah, for his home was there" (1 Sam 7:16,

---

[4] ᵓ*Ag.Ber.* (ed., S. Buber; Krakau, 1902), Perek, נ''ב, 106-107. My translation.

The Mothers and the Rabbis

17). The sixth is Hazzelelponi the mother of Samson, as it is written, "And the name of their sister (Hazlelponit) [Hazleponi] (1 Chron 4:3). This corresponds to the sixth day. What was created on the sixth day? Man. What did Man have? Death at the hands of a woman, as it is written, "And to Adam he said . . ." (Gen 3:17). "So Samson her son died at the hands of a woman in the valley of Sorek, whose name was Delilah" (Judg 16:4). "And the Philistines seized him and gouged out his eyes" (ibid. 16:21). The seventh is Zion, corresponding to the seventh day. What is written of it? "And he rested on the seventh day" (Exod 20:11). And of Zion "This is my resting place forever" (Ps 132:14). Therefore Isaiah said "Sing, O barren one who did not bear (Isa 54:1).

This midrash is an example of the functional category of "enumeration of Scriptural examples" which Towner calls "hermeneutical analogy." Diverse passages are drawn together from all over the Bible and related by means of a common motif. This type, Towner has observed, "tends to be theologically and homiletically directed, rather than aimed at solving exegetical problems."[5] A double analogy is at work in the passage. First, the stories of all of the barren women are brought into relation to each other; this provides the enumeration of Scriptural examples. Second, they are related as a group to the seven days of creation by means of the *Stichwort* seven. This provides two resources for homilies: the ways in which the barren women relate to each other and the ways in which they relate to the creation. The seven days of creation device provides a "plot" and a climactic focus. Just as the seventh day was the climax of creation, so the seventh barren woman will be the climax of the enumeration of Scriptural examples. This intention is announced at the beginning, before the seven days of creation are introduced, when Isa 54:1 is cited in connection with the lemma, "And she vowed a vow . . ." from 1 Sam 1:11. The conclusion is given at the outset, and the midrash then proceeds to demonstrate how that conclusion was reached. Hannah's prayer that God remember her and visit her, which resulted in the birth of Samuel, really applies to Zion, for whom we are praying God to remember and visit.

The midrash works not by relating the barren woman but rather some aspect of her son's life to the creation story. The common motif which provides the analogy between the woman and the day of creation is in

---

[5] *Enumeration*, 120-121.

each case drawn from a passage which relates incidents in the life of the son, well after he has been granted to the barren woman and has grown up. (In the case of Sarah the link is with Abraham rather than with Isaac. This may be because by the first century C.E., Isaac had taken on a special and somewhat eschatological significance, not unlike that of Zion, and so he would not be appropriate as the first member of an enumeration which built up to a climax.)

It is important to recognize that the midrash links the son of the barren woman rather than the woman herself to the creation, because the final member of the enumeration, Zion, is not explained, but its explanation is implicit in the way the first six barren women have been treated. Each day of creation "pre-figured" the life of the son of one of the barren women in Israel. The seventh day therefore prefigured or revealed that God would remember Zion as he had remembered the other barren women.

But Zion is not given a son; she is given Yahweh's presence. The allusion to Ps 132:14 makes the point of the midrash: just as YHWH gave a son to the barren women of the Bible, so he gives his presence to his people in the present. Even in their most barren times, the people are assured of YHWH's intention to dwell with them to give them life.

While this midrash represents a very expanded and complete form of the tradition, the core of the analogy—the linking of the barren women with Zion—is clearly the most significant aspect for homiletical use.

Pesikta de Rab Kahana

This connection between the seven barren mothers is made in *Pesiq. Rab Kah.*, a collection of homilies for festivals and special Sabbaths. In one exposition the stories of the seven are interpreted by means of Ps 113:9; the midrash is structured, as the one from *'Ag.Ber.* is, so that the listener is led up to the climax, which is Zion bearing her sons.

> "Sing o barren one who did not bear" (Isa 54:1). "He gives the barren woman a home, making her the joyous mother of children" (Ps 113:9). There are seven barren ones: Sarah, Rebecca, Rachel, Leah, the wife of Manoah, Hannah, and Zion. Another interpretation: "Giving the barren woman a home"—this is our mother Sarah. "Now Sarah was Barren" (Gen 11:30). "Making her the joyous mother of children"—"Sarah suckled sons" (Gen 21:7). Another interpretation: "Giving the barren woman a home"—this is Rebecca. "And Isaac prayed for his wife Rebecca because she was barren"

(Gen 25:21). "Making her the joyous mother of children"—"And the Lord saw that Leah was hated" (Gen 29:31). From this (we know that) Leah was barren. "Making her the joyous mother of children"—"For I have borne him six sons" (Gen 30:20). Another interpretation: "Giving the barren woman a home"—this is the wife of Manoah. "And the angel of the Lord appeared to the woman and said, 'Behold, you are barren and have no children'" (Judg 13:3). "Making her the joyous mother of children"—"And she conceived and bore three sons and two daughters" (1 Sam 2:21). Another interpretation: "Giving the barren woman a home"—this is Zion. "Sing o barren one who did not bear" (Isa 54:1). "Making her the joyous mother of children"—"Then you will say in your heart, 'Who has borne me these?'" (Isa 49:21).[6]

A line is missing from the text; the ending of the wife of Manoah and the beginning of Hannah have been inadvertently dropped, so that the two stories have been conflated. That this could happen proves the similarity of the stories and the way in which they are treated in the midrash. Each of the seven is interpreted in exactly the same way: the occurrence of the words barren עקרה and children בנים in their stories means that the Psalm verse, which contains those two words, refers to them.

The interest of the midrash is in the barren women as examples of those whom YHWH has raised up from a condition of deprivation and humiliation to a state of being blessed and joyful. The most important of the barren mothers, of course, is Zion, and the position of Zion as number seven in the midrash underlines this. Further, the use of a citation which is in the second person rather than in the third person (Isa 49:21) allows the preacher to address his congregation directly at the end of the midrash. The "you" of the citation would be heard by the people as an address to them, and it moves the midrash out of the recitation of the past gracious acts of God into the contemplation of what he will do in the future.

The stories of the barren women in the midrash are interpreted by Ps 113:9; but this Psalm verse would recall for those who heard it the entire Psalm. Giving the barren woman a home and making he the joyous mother of children is an example in the Psalm of how YHWH looks down upon the earth. The verse just before the one cited in the midrash says "He raises the poor from the dust, and lifts the needy from the ash heap, to make

---

[6] *Pesiq. Rab Kah.* (ed., S. Buber [1898], Perek קמא). My translation.

them sit with princes, with the princes of his people." The connection between the poor and needy and the barren women is implicitly drawn by the midrash. The meticulous, almost monotonous manner in which each woman's story is related to the Psalm verse emphasizes the regularity and trustworthiness of YHWH's gracious acts. The very form of the midrash conveys the homiletical message that YHWH can be counted on to raise the poor from the dust.

Another midrash from *Pesiq. Rab Kah.* uses the barren matriarchs, in a somewhat different way, to teach that YHWH does not fail to raise up his saints.

> "Not comforted" (Isa 54:11). Rabbi Levi said: For every place where it is written "She did not have," there is a place where it is written "She did have." "Now Sarah was barren and did not have a child" (Gen 30:11). She did have: "Sarah suckled children" (Gen 21:7). "Now Peninnah had children, but Hannah did not have children" (1 Sam 1:2). She did have: "And the Lord visited Hannah and she conceived and bore three sons and two daughters" (1 Sam 2:21). "It is Zion, for whom no one cares" (Jer 30:17). She did have: "And he will come to Zion as redeemer" (Isa 59:20). Therefore it says "Sing o barren one who did not bear" (Isa 54:1). And she had children: "And you will say in your heart, 'Who has borne me these?'" (Isa 49:19).[7]

The biblical verses about Sarah, Hannah and Zion can be interpreted by the same principle because they all contain the phrase אין לה. In every case the אין לה is replaced by הוה לה; what the woman did not have was provided by God. Again the examples of Sarah and Hannah are intended to prove the case of Zion, whose fulfillment is still in the future. This midrash suggests a cycle of deprivation and fulfillment, of devastation and redemption, which is in the hands of Yahweh. It presents the biblical stories as a kind of paradigm by which the present and the future can be understood and believed in. In the homiletical setting the message would be: If we are "not comforted" now, if we are like the women who were barren, then we are only in the first part of the cycle of redemption; just as their אין לה was turned to הוה לה by YHWH so will it be with us.

---

[7] Ibid., Perek, קלה. My translation.

In all of the midrashim about the seven barren women, two hermeneutical principles are operative. First, all of the stories are related to each other by some verbal similarity, so that the argument from analogy can be used. All of the stories are assigned the same meaning because they all contain a common element—e.g., the word עקרה or the phrases אין לה and הוה לה or the words עקרה and בנים. The result of reading all seven of the stories together is what Daniel Patte calls "the synthetic view of Scripture and of sacred history."[8] Any one of the barren mothers can be understood as a sign of what God has done for Israel and of what he will do for Israel. As a group they present the entire salvation history "telescoped" around seven figures. As individuals, each bears in her own story the theme of promise and fulfillment which is the theme of Israel's story.

The second hermeneutical principle which is operative is a form of actualization. In every case the last barren mother to be named is Zion, and the reference to her children is a reference to the future. Unlike the first six women, whose sons have been born and are in the past, Zion has not yet borne her sons. While her barrenness is seen in the present, her fruitfulness is yet to come. The promise has been given but it has not yet been fulfilled. The significance of the first six stories in these midrashim is as proof that God will do to the seventh barren one as he has done to them. By telling the stories of the first six in the context of the seventh, the midrash also reinterprets the old stories about the mothers. For the preacher, the significance of the barren women lies not in the past but in the future; the true meaning of those stories is yet to be revealed to Israel when Zion bears her sons.

THE MOTIF OF ANSWERED PRAYER

A second classification of the midrashim in which the barren matriarchs have a significant role can be made of those texts which combine the motif of barrenness with the motif of answered prayer. Unlike the category which dealt with Zion, these midrashim do not share a formal characteristic, like the enumeration of scriptural examples. But like the first group, this group tends to be homiletically oriented and uses the motif of the barren matriarchs for the purpose of demonstrating the efficacy of prayer.

---

[8] *Early Jewish Hermeneutic in Palestine* (Missoula: Scholars, 1975) 67-74. The rabbinic dictum is "interpret the Bible by the Bible."

The Scriptural basis for this tradition is Gen 20:17-18, which tells of Abraham's prayer on behalf of Abimelech and his household, who had been made barren when Abimelech took Sarah as his wife. By the rabbinic principle of textual proximity ("what comes before and what comes after") these verses are linked with Gen 21:1-2 ויעש יהוה לשרה כאשר דבר ויהוה פקד את-שרה כאשר אמר. Why does the Torah tell of Sarah's pregnancy *here*? Because in the preceding verse Abraham's prayer for Abimelech's wife resulted in *her* pregnancy!

This tradition is preserved in a short form in the Targum Pseudo-Jonathan of Gen 21:1

ויי דכיר ית שרה היכמא דאמר ליה ועבד יי
לשרה ניסא היכמא דמליל אברהם בצלותיה על אבימלך

And the Lord remembered Sarah as he had said to her, and the Lord performed a miracle for Sarah just as Abraham had asked in his prayer for Abimelech.[10]

By the addition of five words, the author of Pseudo-Jonathan has changed the focus of the Torah verse from the fulfillment of YHWH's promise to the efficacy of Abraham's prayer. The brevity of the allusion suggests that the author was reminding his audience of a tradition with which they were already familiar. A fuller version of this tradition occurs in *Pesikta Rabbati:*[11]

> When Abraham prayed in behalf of Abimelech and his wife, and all the Philistines conceived and bore children, the angels rose up, complaining: "Master of the Universe, all these years Sarah was barren, and Abimelech's wife was barren." (Whence is it known that Abimelech's wife was barren? Because it is said "And God healed Abimelech and his wife" (Gen 20:17), and no one is ever healed unless he has been previously smitten.) "Now that Abraham has prayed," the angels went on, "Abimelech's wife was remembered; even his maidservants were. These were remembered, but Sarah remains barren. Justice demands that she also be remembered."

---

[10] M. Ginsburger, ed., *Thargum Jonathan ben Usiel zum Pentateuch nach der Londoner Handschrift,* Berlin, 1903 (reprinted 1971).

[11] פסקתא רבתי (ed. M. Friedman; Wien, 1880), מב, translated in William G. Braude, *Pesikta Rabbati* (New Haven: Yale, 1968) 2.743.

The rabbinic interest in Abraham's prayers is joined with the important exegetical principle of "measure for measure": the reward which God metes out for an action will be appropriate to the action. God is bound by his own laws of justice to reward Abraham's good deed for Abimelech in kind.

The tradition of Abraham's prayers is developed further in *Gen. Rab.*:[12]

אברהם היה מתפלל על עקרות והם
נפקדות. ועל החולים והם מרויחים

Abraham used to pray for barren women, and they were remembered; and on behalf of the sick; and they were healed.

The tradition of Abraham, the righteous man whose prayers on behalf of others were heard, not only establishes the figure of Abraham as an especially devout man, but more importantly, these midrashim suggest that if a man prays for others, his own needs will not be overlooked by God.

The prayer of Isaac on behalf of Rebecca in Gen 25:21 also served as the basis of meditation on the prayers of the righteous:

ויעתר יצחק ליהוה לנכח אשתו
כי עקרה הוא

"And Isaac prayed" (Gen 25:21). Rabbi Isaac said: Why are the prayers of the righteous likened to a shovel? Just as the shovel turns the grain on the threshing floor from place to place, so the prayers of the righteous turn the dispensations of the Holy One Blessed be He from dispensations of anger to dispensations of mercy.[13]

The exegetical basis of the midrash is the play on עתיר pray, and עתר, shovel. The underlying assumption, however, is that Isaac's prayer for Rebecca resulted in her pregnancy, and it therefore provides material for preaching about the prayers of the righteous. Just as Isaac's prayer turned barrenness to fruitfulness, so the prayers of the righteous turn divine anger to divine mercy.

In another tradition, Rebecca's pregnancy is attributed to the prayer of Isaac:

---

[12] *Gen. Rab.* לט.
[13] Cited in Jastrow, ספר מלים, p. 1130, from יבמות סד.

> R. Yehuda ben Simon in the name of R. Shimon ben Eleazar said: Why was Rebecca barren? So that the gentiles would not say that she bore fruit easily, as it was said of her "Our sister, may you be the mother of thousands" (Gen 24:60). When Isaac prayed for her she was visited. Thus it is written "And Isaac prayed for his wife" (Gen 25:21).[14]

Another tradition develops the idea that God wished to hear the prayers of the mothers themselves. In a commentary on Cant 2:14, following the above midrash about Rebecca, the question is asked, "Why were the mothers barren"?

> R. Azariah in the name of R. Yohannan bar Pappa said: Why were the mothers barren? So that they would be endeared to their husbands by their beauty. R. Huna and R. Jeremiah in the name of R. Hiya said: Why were the mothers barren? So that they would spend many years without working. R. Huna in the name of R. Meir said: Why were the mothers barren? So that their husbands would take pleasure in them. For when a woman is pregnant she is ungainly and neglected (by her husband). But for all the ninety years that Sarah was not pregnant she was like a bride in the bridal chamber. As soon as she conceived, her good looks were changed. As the Scriptures say elsewhere: In pain you shall bring forth children. R. Levi in the name of R. Sila from k'far T'marta and R. Helab in the name of R. Yohannan said: Why were the mothers barren? On account of the Holy One Blessed be He desiring to hear their thoughts. He said to them, O my dove, why did I make you barren? Because I desired to hear your thoughts. As it is written, "Your voice is sweet and your face is comely" (Cant 2:14).[15]

The midrash leads up to the citation from the Song of Songs, and thereby presents as the strongest argument for the barrenness of the mothers the desire of God to hear their prayers. Another version of the same midrash occurs in *Gen. Rab.*,[16] in which it is said that "The Holy One blessed be he desired their prayers and their supplications." But while the version in *Cant. Rab.* leads up to the desire of God to hear the mothers call upon him, in *Gen. Rab.* the order is the opposite, and the text

---

[14] *Cant. Rab.* בפ. My translation.
[15] Ibid.
[16] *Gen. Rab.* מה.

leads up to the description of Sarah as a bride in the bridal chamber. (The line that her good looks vanished when Isaac was conceived is absent from *Gen. Rab.*) The context is a commentary on Gen 16:2, and the purpose is a defense of Sarah.

These midrashim indicate how one tradition could function in different ways simply by a difference in context and emphasis. The "standard" list of reasons why the mothers were barren could be adapted to a homily on Sarah as easily as to one on prayer. Even when the rabbinic traditions became fixed, they were, like the biblical traditions, adaptable.

It is the story of Hannah, and particularly Hannah's vow in 1 Sam 1:11, which provides the richest source of midrashim on prayer. 1 Sam 1:1-2:10 was the haftarah reading for the first day of New Year according to the Palestinian triennial cycle. In *Pesikta Rabbati*, a collection of homiletical midrashim for the special Sabbaths and feasts of the year, Piska 43 is devoted entirely to 1 Sam 2:21: "So the Lord remembered Hannah and she conceived, and bore three sons and two daughters." This Piska takes the common form of *Yelammedenu rabbenu*, in which a religious problem is posed with the formula "Let our master teach us." The answer to the problem is given, followed by a discourse which relates to the problem in some way, using the Scripture reading for the day.[17] The problem in *Pesikta Rabbati* 43 is: "How far into the month may the blessing for the new moon's advent be recited?" This question leads to a discourse on the recitation of blessings and then of prayer in general.

The lemma is evidence that God does not frustrate the spirit of the righteous by withholding the reward due them. He grants them whatever they desire in keeping with the verse: "He will fulfill the desire of them that fear him" (Ps 145:19). Several midrashim on 1 Sam 1:11 are then introduced with the words:

> To whom else was granted what she desired? To Hannah, who prayed before the Holy One, blessed be He; at the conclusion of her prayer, the Holy One, blessed be He, did not let her go forth empty-handed. For the Holy One, blessed be He heard her prayer and granted her all that she asked of Him.[18]

---

[17]See *Pesiq. R.* (trans. William G. Braude; New Haven: Yale, 1968) 1 1-33, on introductory matters.
[18]פסקתא רבתה (ed., M. Friedman; Wein, 1880), translated in Braude, *Pesiq. R.*, 2.756.

Hannah proves the truth of the Psalm citation, and her case provides teachings on prayer.

Hannah's prayer, which begins יהוה צבאות, is the basis of several midrashim which expand her prayer and develop the theme of importunity in prayer. In one midrash, Hannah reminds God that there is a host above and a host below. The host above do not procreate, eat or drink, or die, while the host below do all of these things. Since she is not procreating, she does not know whether she belongs to the host above or to the host below. If she is of the host below, she should be bearing children.

Another midrash relates that Hannah prayed[19]

רבונו של עולם כל הצבאות האילו ישלך ואין לי אחד בהם

In another version this prayer is expanded with a parable:

> "O Lord of Hosts, if you will indeed look upon the affliction of your maidservant, etc." R. Eleazar said: From the day when the Holy One blessed be He created the world no one called upon the Holy One blessed be He as "Hosts" until he created Hannah and she called him "Hosts." Hannah said to the Holy One blessed be He: "Master of the universe! From all of the myriads of hosts which you have created in your world, is it so difficult for you to give me one son?" To what may this thing be compared? It is like a king of flesh and blood who gave a feast for his servants. A poor man came and stood at the door and said to them, "Give me one broken piece," but they did not pay any attention to him. He pressed, and was brought into the presence of the king, and he said to him, "My master the king! From all the whole feast which you have made, is it so difficult for you to give me one piece"?[20]

The formula משל למה הדבר דומה "To what may this thing be compared?" signals the beginning of a parable, a common literary device in the rabbinic literature. Particularly the meeting between the king and the poor man, both stock characters of early Jewish midrash, is a favorite theme, and the outcome of the story does not even need to be told. Whenever a man who is rich, powerful or wise is approached by one who is poor, humble and simple, the reader knows that the wise man is about to be

---

[19]Piska מג.
[20]ספר האגדה Vol. 1, p. פה. My translation.

The Mothers and the Rabbis

instructed by the simple man. Underlying the parable is the affirmation that the just cause of a righteous man will be heard by God, because God himself abides by the rules of the Torah.

The motif of the justice of Hannah's cause emboldening her prayer occurs in another midrash:

> R. Jose ben Zimra said: על-לבה. Upon her heart: She said to the Holy One blessed be He: Master of the universe, of all that you have created in woman, you have not created anything in vain. The eyes for seeing, the ears for hearing, the nose for breathing, the mouth for speaking, the hands for doing work, the feet for walking, the breasts for nursing. The breasts which you have placed *upon my heart*—for what? Are they not for nursing? Give me a son and I will nurse with them![21]

The midrash is based on a play on the words על-לבה from the text of 1 Sam 1:13, which mean idiomatically "to herself" but which are interpreted literally as "upon her heart" in order to make them refer to Hannah's breasts. The midrash is playful, and clearly the rabbis enjoyed themselves in their clever and fanciful interpretations of simple biblical idioms. Nevertheless, underlying this midrash, as also the one preceding it, is the principle that the straightforward and unassailable logic of Hannah's argument made her case irresistible. Of course the thought of the Holy One blessed be He being instructed by a woman on the nature of His creation would have delighted the rabbis. One senses that part of the rabbinic doctrine of God held that he is a good sport.

The concept of prayer as negotiating with God is not new in Jewish tradition. It is known from Gen 18:22-33; although the biblical text does not mention prayer, the term ויגש and the intercessory nature of Abraham's request made it easy for interpreters to place this scene in the category of prayer. This kind of negotiating and discussing with God as part of prayer is a form of importunity; if God is not convinced by the argument, then he will be worn down by the persistence of the person praying and will grant the request. This concept of prayer can be found in the teaching on prayer in Luke 11:1-3, indicating that it was established by the first century C.E. Like the rabbis, Luke accompanies his teaching with a parable of a man asking a friend for food, and like the king in the

---

[21] ספר האגדה, Vol. 1, p פה. My translation.

rabbinic parables, the man with the food is unable to deny the request of the suppliant, just as God is unable to deny the prayers of his people.

The midrashim about Hannah's prayers are intended to illustrate the teaching that prayer is efficacious, that God listens to the prayers of the righteous and answers them. This motif is part of the New Year theme of God's mercy and compassion toward Israel. The festivals of New Year, the Sabbath of repentence and the Day of Atonement together form a season of reconciliation with God. At the heart of the Piskas for the season is the belief that God has been merciful to those who, like the mothers and fathers of the Torah, remind God that they are waiting for him. The Torah reading of Gen 21:1 with the Haftarah of 2 Sam 2:21 both refer to God remembering and visiting women who were waiting for him. In both cases the action of God is viewed not as a surprise or even as an act of God's initiative, but is rather the fulfillment of his word, a sign of his faithfulness and his response to the prayers of his faithful ones. He visited Sarah *as he had said* and as Abraham had spoken in his prayer on behalf of Abimelech. He visited Hannah *in response to her prayer*. By relating the motif of response to prayer with the motif of the faithfulness of God's word, the rabbis were able to establish their teaching that God heard the prayers of the righteous on the authority of the Torah teaching that God was faithful to his word.

It is significant that the midrashim cited above were heard on New Year's Day, at the time when men's fortunes for the coming year are determined in heaven. If New Year's Day is a time of praying and of relying on God's mercy, then the homiletical exposition of stories in which God hears prayers would be a very significant part of the liturgy. Sarah and Hannah function as signs of God's mercy and of his faithfulness; that is, of his willingness to listen to the prayers of his people, especially at the New Year.

THE MOTIF OF RAISING UP THE LOWLY

Closely related to the homiletical interest in the barren matriarch stories as examples of answered prayer is the homiletical interest in them as illustrations of the principle that God raises up the humble and vindicates the righteous. A verse from the prophets or the writings usually provided a general statement by which the story from the Torah was interpreted, indicating again the liturgical origins of the midrash.

"And the Lord saw that Leah was hated, and he opened her

The Mothers and the Rabbis

womb" (Gen 29:31). "For the Lord hearkened unto the needy, and despiseth not His prisoners" (Ps 69:34). R. Benjamin ben Levi said: The beginning of this verse does not match its end, nor the end the beginning. The verse should surely have read either, "For the Lord hearkeneth unto the needy and despiseth not *the* prisoners," or "For the Lord hearkeneth to His needy and despiseth not His prisoners." But, "For the Lord hearkeneth unto the needy," refers to Israel, for R. Johannan said, Wherever "poor," "afflicted" or "needy" occurs, Scripture refers to Israel. "And despiseth not His prisoners" alludes to the childless women who are prisoners in their houses, but as soon as the Holy One blessed be He visits them with children, they become erect. The proof is that Leah was hated in her house, yet when God visited her she became erect; hence it is written, "And the Lord saw that Leah was hated, and he opened her womb" (Gen 29:31).[22]

The verse from Psalm 69 is linked to Gen 29:31 through the similarity of the words hated (שנואה) and despises (בזה). The parallel members of the Psalm are interpreted as two distinct groups: the needy represents Israel, and the prisoners represent the childless women. That God did not despise his prisoners (Leah) proves also that he listens to the needy (Israel). The real interest of the midrash, therefore, is hinted at in the line "Whenever poor, afflicted or needy occurs, Scripture refers to Israel." It is in relation to the affliction of Israel that Leah's affliction becomes significant. Yet the conclusion is implied rather than stated; the reader must supply the final step of the midrash for himself. The point of the midrash is that if God did not despise Leah, the hated wife, all the more will he not despise Israel, his beloved. In a homiletical setting, this point is made more eloquently by analogy than by explicit statement. The technique of leading up to a point and then leaving it unstated is characteristic of the homiletical midrashim, and it is an effective preaching technique.

The same technique is used in another midrashim, also concerning Leah, to demonstrate the care of God for the lowly:

סומך יי לכל הנופלים. אלו העקרות שהם נופלים
בתוך בתיהם. וזוקף לכל הכפופים. כיון שהקב''ה
פוקדן בבנים הן נזקפות.

---

[22]*Bereshit Rabba* 71.1. Translated in *Gen. Rab.* (trans. H. Freedman and M. Simon; London: Soncino, 1939) 2.652.

תדע לך שכן לאה שנואת הבית היתה וכיון
שפקדה הקב"ה נזקפה.
הה"ד וירא יי כי שנואה לאה

"The Lord upholdeth all that fall" (Ps 145:14)—viz. childless women who fall [i.e., are disgraced] in their homes; "And raiseth up all those that are bowed down" (ibid.): as soon as God visits tham with children, they are raised up. The proof is that Leah was hated in her house, yet when the Holy One blessed be He visited her, she was raised up. Thus it is written, "And the Lord saw that Leah was hated ..." (Gen 29:31).[23]

Again the general statement of the Psalm verse is "proved" by the particular example of Leah. The use of נזקפות "raised up" in both midrashim about Leah, though it occurs only in Ps 145:14 and not in the Psalm cited in the other midrash about Leah, indicates an accepted tradition that Leah was נזקפה. The first midrash was therefore able to draw on the association of Ps 145:14 with Leah without explicitly stating the source. In both cases, Leah is a sign: if God raised up Leah, who was hated, how much more will he raise up Israel, whom he loves.

Sarah also serves as a sign that God raises up the lowly, and that he keeps his word. Gen 21:1, particularly, is the proof text for the idea that God keeps his word to the humble. In *Gen. Rab.* the discussion of Gen 21:1 opens with a citation of Ezek 17:24:

> And all the trees of the field shall know that I the Lord have brought down the high tree, have exalted the low tree, have dried up the green tree, and have made the dry tree to flourish, I the Lord have spoken and have done it.[24]

The high tree is interpreted as Abimelech, the low tree is Abraham, the green tree refers to Abimelech's wives and the dry tree is Sarah. The birth of Isaac, God doing to Sarah as he had spoken, is evidence that God exalts the humble, just as the punishment given to Abimelech (Gen 20:18) is evidence that he brings down the mighty.

---

[23] Ibid.
[24] *Bereshit Rabba* 53.1. Translated in Freedman, *Gen. Rab.* 1.461.

In another exposition of Gen 21:1 Sarah's pregnancy is a reward for her humility:

> And just as whoever abuses his fellow man is punished, so you find that anyone who, like Sarah, abases himself, will receive his reward. For she said: "Behold now, the Lord hath restrained ME from bearing" (Gen 16:2). The Holy One, blessed be He, thereupon declared: Because thou didst abase thyself, saying "The Lord hath restrained ME"—thee, as thou livest not Abraham—I shall particularly remember. And the proof of His remembering? The verse read in the lesson for the day "And the Lord remembered SARAH as He has said."[25]

By calling herself barren rather than Abraham, Sarah "abases" herself. The theme of rivalry between husband and wife over the question of who is the barren one is found in Josephus and in Pseudo-Philo, in elaborations on the story of Samson's birth.[26]

In *Gen. Rab.*, Sarah's pregnancy is a reward for her good deeds:

> R. Adda said: The Holy One, blessed be He, is a trustee פקדונות: Amalek deposited with Him bundles of thorns [wrong-doings]; therefore he returned to him bundles of thorns [punishment], as it says, "I remember that which Amalek did to Israel (1 Sam 15:2). Sarah laid up with Him a store of pious acts and good deeds; therefore the Lord returned her [the reward for these,] as it says, "And the Lord remembered פקד Sarah" (Gen 21:1).[27]

Here a play on the word פקד is the basis of the midrash; God visits according to the deeds which people store up with Him and is therefore a trustee of rewards and punishments.

In both of these midrashim the homiletical point is that Sarah remained humble and righteous throughout the period of her barrenness and was rewarded by God, who kept his word and visited her. The biblical narratives make no reference to good deeds or to Isaac's birth as a reward; on the contrary, the Yahwist emphasized the graciousness of Yahweh in spite

---

[25] *Pesiq. R.* 42. Translated in Braude, *Pesikta Rabbati* 2.747.
[26] Josephus, *The Jewish Antiquities*, Book 5. *The Biblical Antiquities of Pseudo-Philo*, XLII.
[27] *Gen. Rab.*, נג. My translation.

of the failings of both Sarah and Abraham. This is possible because of the atomistic exegesis of the rabbis. By this principle, individual words of the biblical texts are more significant than the overall context; so the midrash from *Pesiq. R.* is based on interpreting the word "me," while the midrash above is based on the word "remember," פקד. In the second case the argument is based on the principle of *Gezerah Shawah*, or inference by analogy. The same word, פקד is used in the passage about Amalek and in the passage about Sarah; because Amalek deserved the visitation he received, so Sarah must have also deserved the visitation she received.

The motif of the exaltation of the humble is seen also in the midrashim which link Zion with the six "mothers" and indicates that Zion, like them, will be the mother of important sons. The use of Ps 113:9 in relation to Zion especially underlines the motif of raising up the lowly.

In the development of traditions about the individual mothers, the theme of vindication begins to be more important than the theme of raising up the lowly. In *Pesiq. R.* we read that for each child born to Hannah, one of Peninnah's children died. The story of the birth of Isaac becomes increasingly miraculous and surrounded by stories of the vindication of Abraham and Sarah before the gentiles. One of these is instructive about the way in which the tradition was used:

> "And she said, 'Who would have said to Abraham that Sarah would suckle sons?'" (Gen 21:7)). Why does it say that Sarah suckled *sons*? R. Levi said: On the very day that Abraham weaned Isaac his son he made a great feast. All the gentiles of the world were murmuring and saying "See the old man and old woman; they have brought in a foundling from the market place and are saying that it is their son! Not only that, but they are making a great feast in order to prove their words!" What did Abraham our father do? He went and invited all of the leaders of the time and Sarah our mother invited their wives. One by one each brought her son with her, but not their wet-nurses. A miracle was done through Sarah our mother: her breasts were opened like two fountains and she nursed all of them. They passed by and were murmuring and saying: "If Sarah who is ninety has given birth, has Abraham who is a hundred begotten?" At once the face of Isaac was changed and became like Abraham's. They all realized and said, "Abraham has begotten Isaac."[28]

---

[28] *B.Meṣ.* פז. Cited in ספר האגדה. The tradition of Sarah's miraculous nursing is reported also in *Gen. Rab.* 53, *Pesiq. R.* 43 and *Yal.* (Wayyera).

It is not enough that Abraham and Sarah have a son; the miracle must be elaborated and expanded. The tradition of Sarah nursing the sons of the elite women of the time occurs in several places, usually with the purpose of vindicating Sarah, and with the conclusion that the sons whom she nursed became proselytes. The image of Sarah nursing children who later became proselytes may have been suggested by the tradition of Jerusalem as mother nursing an entire people. The link between Sarah and Jerusalem was explored early in the development of the barren matriarch midrashim, and it is characteristic of Jewish haggadic tradition that a motif attached to one barren woman would be transferred to another. In Isa 66:10-14 Jerusalem nurses her sons in order that "it shall be known that the hand of the Lord is with his servants." The miracle done through Sarah's breasts functions in the same way in the haggadic tradition: it proves that the hand of the Lord is with his servants the Jews.

THE MOTIF OF THE WORLD TO COME

In several midrashic traditions the remembrance of barren women is a sign of the world to come. This tradition is not as common as the traditions of answered prayer and of raising the humble, but because of its use in the New Testament, it is nonetheless significant.

In *Gen. Rab.* 77, 1 some of the signs of the world to come are enumerated:

> The Holy One, blessed be He, anticipated in this world through the agency of the righteous everything that He will do in the Hereafter. Thus God will resurrect the dead, and Elijah resurrected the dead; God shuts up the rain, and Elijah shut up the rain; God will bless the little, and Elijah blessed the little. God resurrects the dead and Elisha resurrects the dead; God remembered childless women and Elisha remembered childless women.

The reference to the childless woman is to the Shunammite woman in 2 Kings 4 who is given the gift of a son in return for her hospitality to the prophet. According to the midrash, the birth of her son was an anticipation of the world to come.

That the barren will bear in the world to come is also indicated in *Pesiq. R.* 42,4:

> R. Judah the sons of R. Simon, citing R. Hanin in the name of

R. Samuel the son of Isaac said: All barren women everywhere in the world were remembered together with Sarah and were with child at the same time she was; and when she gave birth to a child, all of them gave birth to children at the same time she did. It was for this reason that Sarah said: "God hath given me occasion for laughter; every one that heareth will laugh in joy with me" (Gen 21:6). It is a question, however, whether a person's laughter—Reuben's, say—is necessarily an occasion for someone else like Simeon, busy in the field with his cutting tool, to laugh with him, unless the same good thing has befallen both men. Even so, in saying that all who heard Sarah laugh, laughed with her, Scripture means that barren women everywhere in the world were remembered at the same time she was: "And the Lord remembered others along with Sarah."

And not only this remembrance, but much more besides. When Sarah bore her child, every blind man in the world was given sight; every cripple was made straight; every mute was given speech; and every madman was healed of his madness.[29]

The healing of the blind, the cripples and the mute and mad were well known as eschatological signs, at least by the first century C.E. Further, this midrash is immediately followed by one which says that at Isaac's birth the light of the sun was intensified to the magnitude of the original light of creation, which would not happen again until the beginning of the world to come. The image of the primeval light is clearer in Piska 23,6, where it is said that the primeval light, created on the first day of creation, enabled Adam to see from one end of the world to the other. But after the disobedience of Adam, and the "wicked deeds" of Genesis 4-11, God hid the primeval light and holds it ready for the righteous in the world to come. The brilliance of the light at Isaac's birth, then, like the healing of all barren woman, the restoration of sight to the blind, and of speech to the mute, as well as the healing of other bodily infirmities, is a foreshadowing of the world to come. By setting the healing of Sarah's barrenness in such a context, and by invoking such traditionally known eschatological signs, the aggadists intended their listeners to connect the healing of Sarah's barrenness and the birth of Isaac with the signs of the world to come.

---

[29] *Pesiq. R.* 42, translated in Braude, *Pesiq. R.* 2.745. See also *Gen. Rab.* 53 and *Yal.* (Wayyera).

The Mothers and the Rabbis 137

CONCLUSIONS

We have seen four ways in which the barren matriarch stories functioned in rabbinic preaching: (1) to relate Zion's future with the matriarchs' stories; (2) to teach about prayer; (3) to indicate that Yahweh raises up the humble and vindicates the righteous; and (4) to be a sign of the world to come. Two of these four functions are found already in the Hebrew Bible, indicating that the rabbinic developments of the tradition were based on biblical developments. But the rabbis did not simply use biblical traditions; they also used biblical *principles of interpretation*. They did not say exactly what the biblical authors said, but they interpreted the stories in some of the same ways in which the biblical authors interpreted them.

Second Isaiah used the story of Sarah's barrenness as a paradigm for Zion and for the future of the people Israel. For both Second and Third Isaiah the real import of the barren matriarch stories is not in the past but in the future: what God did for Sarah is evidence of what he will do for his exiled people. This use of the ancient stories as a paradigm for the future is precisely what we saw in (1) above. Here the individual Sarah functions as a mirror for the whole people. For the rabbis, the signficance of Sarah's story is in its relation to Zion's story.

The story of Hannah, as we have seen, is interpreted by the Song of Hannah, so that Hannah is a type of the *anawim*, the poor and downtrodden whom Yahweh will raise up. Just as the authors of 1 Samuel 1-3 interpreted Hannah as a symbol of the whole people in affliction, so the rabbis interpret the barren women as symbols of the afflicted and hated whom Yahweh visits. In both cases the women are used as symbols of the entire group of people, and in both cases the bias of Yahweh for the little people and the humble is assumed.

The use of the barren matriarch tradition as a sign of Yahweh's transformation of this world into the world to come began in the literature of the apocrypha and pseudipigrapha, as we have seen. The same principle as in (1) above is assumed: the significance of the biblical stoies lies not in the past but in the future. For the prophets that future was to be part of Israel's history; for the author of the Apocalypse of Ezra that future was Yahweh's transformation of Jerusalem, and for the rabbis that future was the world to come. While these concepts are by no means identical, the same hermeneutical principle has been employed: the significance of the biblical stories is in their meaning for the future rather than the past.

The function of the barren matriarch stories described in (2) above is not drawn from the biblical or pseudepigraphal writings, but is unique to the rabbinic literature. In using the barren matriarchs to teach about prayer the rabbis use them as models of the faithful and pious Jew. In this use of the tradition, which is the furthest from the biblical witness, we see the greatest amount of legend and haggadic development. The prayer of Hannah is expanded and played upon, and Abraham is portrayed as a generous and pious man. It is in the prayer midrashim that we see the rabbinic characteristics of playfulness, exegetical ingenuity and free use of legendary elements most clearly. In these midrashim we see, too, the remarkable ability of the rabbis to use the Scriptures to answer the needs of the community.

The most significant difference between the rabbinic use of the barren matriarch stories to teach about prayer and the biblical functions of the stories is the hermeneutic. In using the stories to teach about prayer and humility, the rabbinic interpreters have turned the characters of the stories into models. Sarah, Abraham amd Hannah become models of the faithful Jews, examples to be imitated by the members of the community. While the Scriptures indicate that Sarah, Abraham and the rest of the cast were granted sons because of the graciousness of Yahweh, and as part of his plan for Israel, the rabbis suggest that they were granted sons as a result of their prayers. While in the biblical stories the initiative is always Yahweh's and the barrenness of the women seems to be all part of his plan, in the rabbinic midrasim the barrenness of the women is a problem which Yahweh and the characters involved deal with together. And, in every case, the childless man or woman initiates action by a prayer to Yahweh. Further, while the biblical authors indicate that the matriarchs were granted sons in spite of their deeds, the rabbis suggest that they were given sons because of their righteousness. The Yahwist had specifically rejected this idea in his reinterpretation of the ancient hospitality narrative, in which the old man and woman were rewarded by the gods for their hospitality. For the Yahwist, the son was precisely not a reward but a gift. We might say that in this case the Yahwist uses a hermeneutic of "grace" while the rabbis use one of "works."

The difference between the biblical stories and the rabbinic stories is in the questions each is addressing. The biblical stories are addressing the questions of who Yahweh is and who Israel is; the rabbis are addressing the question of how one should pray and how he should live. It is the difference between *muthos* and *ethos*, in the language of J. A. Sanders, the question "who are we?" and the question "what are we to do?"[30]

---

[30]See "Torah and Christ," in *Int* 29 (1975) 372-90 and on the relation

The Mothers and the Rabbis

How did the rabbis arrive at such a different interpretation of the stories? They applied a new hermeneutical principle to the biblical stories, because they were using them to answer a new question. However, the basis for their interpretation is present in the biblical material; it is in the way they use it that we see a change. The idea that Yahweh hears and answers prayers is certainly present: he hears Isaac's prayer for Rebecca (Gen 25:21); he listens to Leah (Gen 30:17); remembers Rachel (Gen 30:22); and most clearly, he hears Hannah. Hannah's prayer, Eli's blessing ("May the Lord grant your petition"), the words "the Lord remembered her," and Hannah's interpretation of the birth ("For this child I prayed; and the Lord has granted me my petition which I made to him") all strengthen the motif of answered prayer. Further, Hannah and Elkanah are clearly righteous and faithful people (in contrast to Peninnah), a motif which is absent from the narratives about the women in Genesis.

But while the motif of answered prayer is present in the narrative, it is not the central interest of the editor. The Song of Hannah, which interprets the narrative, is about the graciousness of Yahweh who lifts up the poor, feeds the hungry and gives children to the barren. Hannah is not a model to be imitated but a sign of Yahweh's graciousness and of his care for Israel.

The rabbis have used two principles of interpretation which are not biblical. First, they have conflated all of the stories together; the differences which we have noted between the story of Hannah and the stories of the women in Genesis are not recognized. The motif of Hannah's prayer has colored the interpretation of the stories of the other childless people in the Bible. Secondly, the rabbis have presented the biblical characters as models of the faithful Jew, to be followed and imitated by Jews in their own time. Hannah's persistence, Abraham's intercessory prayer, Rachel's calling on Yahweh all are seen as models of Jews at prayer. They are proof that Yahweh hears the prayers of his faithful; if people will only pray in the same way and be faithful in their lives, they, too, will be rewarded by Yahweh.[31]

---

between midrashic and mishnaic interpretations, see *Early Jewish Hermeneutic in Palestine* 109-115.
[31] The change in emphasis in interpreting the Torah is very interesting and not entirely understood. Sanders argues that the change came in late Persian or Hellenistic times, partly in response to the challenges to Hellenism (see his "Torah" in *IDBSup* 909-911). This focus on *ethos* rather than *muthos* was sharpened after 70 AD with the loss of the Temple and the establishment of Pharisaic hegemony.

Epilogue

The barren matriarch tradition was continually reinterpreted from the tenth century B.C.E. through the first century C.E. These reinterpretations occurred in many different literary genres and contexts, and they functioned in different ways. Common to all of them, however, is the fact that the ancient tradition was able to be adapted to new contexts and to speak in significant ways to the needs of the diverse communities of ancient Israel and early Judaism, particularly in times of crisis and transition. This study has tried to show the continuity between the formation of the barren matriarch tradition within the biblical literature and the continual adaptation of the tradition in early Judaism. But if the work has answered questions about the development of this tradition and its function in the communities of early Judaism, it has also raised new questions.

First, if there is such continuity between the resignification of traditions in biblical and post-biblical times, what is the significance of canonization? If the same process characterized the development of biblical traditions and the continual reinterpretation of these traditions after canonization, why did canonization occur at the points which it did? What difference does it make in the continuing resignification of Israel's early traditions? Was the process of canonization affected by the processes of interpretation in the early Jewish communities? Our work suggests that it was, that what was canonized was not only a corpus of literature but also the principles which were operative in the formation of that literature. Perhaps canonization was intended not so much to fix the limits of the official literature as to set the parameters by which the traditions, already authoritative in their own right, were to be adapted. More studies are needed before we can understand the processes by which the Torah, the Prophets and the Writings were canonized.

Secondly, there are by-ways which this work could not pursue, but which deserve further attention. One of these is the image of Rachel mourning for her sons in Jeremiah 31:15. Is this personification of the people as desolate mother related to the personifications of Jerusalem as the barren woman? In 4 Ezra Jerusalem is portrayed as a woman who was first barren, then bereft of the son she had been given. In what ways does the Rachel tradition function in Second Temple Judaism, and is it related, either historically or functionally, to the barren matriarch tradition?

Another by-way which can be pursued is the tradition of the Church as mother. This tradition is adumbrated already in Gal 4:26, where Paul applies the image of Jerusalem as mother to the early Christian communities. Certainly Revelation 12 and 21 are part of this development. In these texts the motif of Jerusalem as mother appears to develop independently of the barren matriarch tradition. We have seen how deeply rooted the tradition of Jerusalem as mother is in the barren matriarch tradition. Why was the barren matriarch motif dropped from the developing tradition of the Church as mother? Was the barrenness motif remembered only in time of devastation or transition?

Finally, the work indicates the need for more studies in comparative midrash. It is by studying the functions of an individual tradition in the literature of early Judaism that we can best understand the hermeneutical principles and exegetical procedures of these groups. We have seen how the resignification of the barren matriarch tradition in the communities of early Judaism provides us with clues to the self-understanding of the communities. This study is presented as a small part of the complex task of understanding early Jewish exegesis. More studies of how individual traditions functioned in Second Temple Judaism are needed to deepen our understanding of this period which was so formative for both the Church and the Synagogue. If this work stimulates further studies in comparative midrash, it will have achieved a good part of its goal.

Bibliography

Ahlstrom, G. W. *Aspects of Syncretism in Israelite Religion.* Lund: Gleerup, 1963.

Albright, W. F. *Archaeology and the Religion of Israel.* Baltimore: Johns Hopkins, 1968.

―――― *From the Stone Age to Christianity.* New York: Doubleday, 1957.

―――― *Yahweh and the Gods of Canaan.* Garden City: Doubleday, 1969.

Baer, R.A. *Philo's Use of the Categories Male and Female.* Leiden: Brill, 1970.

Bailey, John A. "Initiation of the Primal Woman in Gilgamesh and Genesis 2-3," *JBL* 89 (1970) 137-150.

Bialik and Rabinitzky. *Sefer ha-aggadah.* Tel Aviv: Dvir, n.d.

Bietenhard, H. *Die himmlische Welt im Urchristentum und Judentum.* Tübingen: Mohr, 1951.

Blau, Joseph L. "Tradition and Innovation." In *Essays on Jewish Life and Thought,* ed. J. L. Blau, Philip Friedman, Arthur Hertzberg, Isaac Mendelsohn. New York: Columbia University, 1959.

Blenkinsopp, Joseph. *Prophecy and Canon.* Notre Dame. University of Notre Dame, 1977.

Bloch, Renee. "Midrash," *DBSup* 5 (1957).

Bonnard, P. *L'Epitre de Saint Paul aux Galates.* Paris: Delachaux & Niestle, 1933.

Bonnard, P. E. *Le Second Isaiae.* Paris: Librairie Lecoffre, 1972.

Bostrom, G. *Proverbiastudien: Die Weisheit und das fremde Weib in Spr. 1-9.* Lund: Gleerup, 1935.

Bourke, J. "Samuel and the Ark: A Study in Contrasts," *Dominican Studies* 7 (1954) 73-103.

Bowker, John. *The Targums and Rabbinic Literature.* Cambridge: University Press, 1969.

Box, G. H. *The Ezra-Apocalypse.* London: Pittman, 1912.

Braude, W. G. *Pesikta Rabbati.* New Haven: Yale, 1968.

Brederek, E. *Konkordanz zum Targum Onkelos.* Gissen: Töpelmann, 1906.

Breugemann, Walter. "Next Steps in Tradition Criticism," *Int* 32 (1978) 89-92.

Bright, John. *A History of Israel.* Philadelphia: Westminster, 1975.

Brooks, B. A. "Fertility Cult Functionaries in the O.T.," *JBL* 60 (1941) 227-54.

Brown, R. E. *The Gospel According to John.* Garden City: Doubleday, 1966.

_____ *The Birth of the Messiah.* Garden City: Doubleday, 1977.

Bruno, D. A. *Das Hebraische Epos.* Uppsala: Almquist & Wiksells, 1935.

Buber, S. *Agadath Bereshith: Midraschische Auslegungen zum Ersten Buche Mosis.* New York: Menora, 1959.

_____ *Agadischer Kommentar zum Pentateuch.* Vienna: Fanto, 1893.

_____ *Midrasch Tanchuma: Ein Agadischer Kommentar zum Pentateuch von Rabbi Tanchuma ben Rabbi Abba.* Wilna: Romm, 1888; Jerusalem: Ortsel, 1963.

_____ *Pesikta de Rab Kahana.* Wilna: Romm, 1898.

Callaway, M. C. "The Mistress and the Maid: Midrashic Traditions Behind Gal. 4:21-31." In *Radical Religion Reader: The Bible and Liberation,* ed. Gottwald and Wire. Berkeley: Community for Religious Research and Education, 1976.

Carlson, R. A. *David, the Chosen King.* Uppsala: Almquist & Wiksells, 1964.

Charles, R. H. *The Apocrypha and Pseudepigrapha of the OT.* Oxford: Clarendon, 1913.

Bibliography

Charlesworth, James. *The Pseudepigrapha and Modern Research.* Missoula: Scholars, 1976.

Childs, Brevard. *Myth and Reality in the Old Testament.* London: SCM, 1960.

Childs, Brevard. "Midrash and the O.T." In *Understanding the Sacred Text,* ed. John Reumann. Philadelphia: Fortress, 1972.

Coats, G. W. "Widow's Rights: A Crux in the Structure of Gen. 38," *CBQ* 34 (1972) 461-466.

Colson, F. H., and G. H. Whitaker. *Philo* (in twelve volumes). Loeb Classical Library. Cambridge: Harvard, 1971.

Conzelman, Hans. "The Mother of Wisdom." In *The Future of Our Religious Past,* ed. J. M. Robinson. New York: Harper & Row, 1971.

Dahl, Nils. *The Crucified Messiah.* Minneapolis: Augsburg, 1974.

Danielou, J. *Les Evangiles de l'Enfance.* Paris: Seuil, 1967.

Daube, David. "Rabbinic Methods of Interpretation and Hellenistic Rhetoric," *HUCA* 22 (1950) 239-264.

de Boer, P. A. H. *Second Isaiah's Message.* Leiden: Brill, 1956.

de Lubac, Henri. *The Splendor of the Church.* New York: Sheed and Ward, 1956.

de Vaux, Roland. "Jerusalem et les prophetes," *RB* 73 (1966) 485.

Doeve, J.W. *Jewish Hermeneutics in the Synoptic Gospels and Acts.* Netherlands: van Gorcum, 1954.

Driver, G. R. "Hebrew Mothers," *ZAW* 67 (1955) 246-48.

Duhm, Bernhard. *Das Buch Jesaia.* Göttingen: Vandenhoeck und Ruprecht, 1922.

Dus, J. "Die Geburtslegende Samuels 1 Sam. 1," *RSO* 43 (1968) 163-194.

Eissfeldt, Otto. "Jacob-Lea und Jacob-Rahel," *Kleine Schriften.* Tübingen: J. C. B. Mohr, 1968.

Eliade, M. "Mother Earth and the Cosmic Hierogamies," *Myths, Dreams and Mysteries.* New York, 1960.

Etheridge, J. W. *The Targum Onkelos and Jonathan ben Uzziel on the Pentateuch with Fragments to the Jerusalem Targum.* New York: Ktav, 1968.

Exum, Cheryl. "Literary Patterns in the Samson Saga." Unpublished dissertation, Columbia University, 1976.

Feuillet, Andre. "La messie et sa mere d'apres le chapitre xii de l'Apocalypse," *RB* 66 (1959) 55-86.

Fitzgerald, Aloysius. "The Mythological Background for the Presentation of Jerusalem as a Queen and False Worship in the O.T.," *CBQ* 34 (1972) 403-16.

_____ "*BTWLT* and *BT* as Titles for Capital Cities," *CBQ* 37 (1975) 167-183.

Fohrer, Georg. *Das Buch Jesaja*. Stuttgart: Zwingli Vrlag Zurich, 1964.

Freedman, H., and M. Simon. *Midrash Rabba*. London: Soncino, 1939.

Friedmann, M. *Pesikta Rabbati*. Vienna, 1880.

Gelin, Albert. *The Poor of Yahweh*. Collegeville: Liturgical Press, 1964.

Goff, B. L. "Syncretism in the Religion of Israel," *JBL* 58 (1939) 151-161.

Gray, G. B. *A Critical and Exegetical Commentary on the Book of Isaiah*. New York: Scribner, 1912.

Grelot, P. "La naissance d'Isaac et celle de Jésus," *NRT* 94 (1972) 463-77.

Gunkel, Hermann. *Genesis*. Göttingen, 1922.

Habel, Norman. "An Appeal to Ancient Tradition as a Literary Form," *SBLASP* 1972, 34-54.

Harrelson, Walter. "Guilt and Rites of Purification Related to the Fall of Jerusalem in 587 B.C.," *Numen* 15 (1968) 218-20.

_____ *From Fertility Cult to Worship*. Garden City: Doubleday, 1969.

_____ "Worship in Early Israel," *Biblical Research* 3 (1968) 1-14.

Haupt, Paul. "The Prototype of the Magnificat," *ZDMG* (1904) 617-632.

Hertzberg, Hans W. *I and II Samuel*. Philadelphia: Westminster, 1964.

Hylander, Ivan. *Die Literarische Samuel-Saul Komplex*. Uppsala: Almquist & Wiksell, 1932.

Bibliography 147

Hyman, A. ספר תורה הכתובה והמסור 'ה על תורה נביאים וכתובים. Tel Aviv: Dvir, 1964/65.

Jacob, B. *Das Erste Buch der Torah:* Genesis. Berlin: Schocken, 1934.

James, E. O. *The Cult of the Mother-Goddess.* New York: Praeger, 1959.

Jastrow, M. *A Dictionary of the Targums, the Talmud Babli and Yerushalmi, and the Midrashic Literature.* New York: Pardes, 1950.

Kabisch, A. *Das vierte Buch Esra.* Göttingen: Vandenhöeck und Ruprecht, 1889.

Kadushin, M. *The Rabbinic Mind.* New York: Bloch, 1972.

Kasouski, H. J. *Concordance to the Targum Onkelos.* Jerusalem: Rabbi Cook Foundation, 1939/40.

Ketter, P. *Die Samuelbucher.* Breisgau: Herder, 1940.

Kilian, R. *Die Vorpriestlichen Abrahams-überlieferungen.* Bonn: Peter Hanstein, 1966.

Kissane, E. J. *The Book of Isaiah.* Diblin: Browne & Nolan, 1941.

Knight, Douglas, A. *Rediscovering the Traditions of Israel.* Missoula: Scholars, 1975.

_____. Ed. *Tradition and Theology in the Old Testament.* Philadelphia: Fortress, 1977.

Köhler, Ludwig. *Hebrew Man.* New York: Abingdon, 1966.

Lagrange, M. *St. Paul: Epitre aux Galates.* Paris: Gabalda, 1950.

Le Déaut, Roger. "Traditions targumiques dans le corpus paulinien?" *Bib* 42 (1961) 28-48.

_____. "Apropos A Definition of Midrash," *Int* 25 (1971) 259-84.

Legrande, L. "Fécondité virginal selon l'Esprit dans le Nouveau Testament," *NRT* 84 (1962) 785-805.

Lewy, J. "The Old West-Semitic Sun-God Hammu," *HUCA* 18 (1944) 429-481.

Lietzmann, Hans. *An die Galater.* Tübingen: J. C. B. Mohr, 1971.

Loretz, O. "K‛t ḥyh—'wie jetzt ums Jahr' Gen 18:10," *Bib* 43 (1962) 75-78.

Louise-Henry, Marie. *Jahwist und Priesterschrift.* Calwer, 1960.

Lyonnet, S. "S. Paul et l'exegese juive de son temps," *Melanges A. Robert.* Paris: Bloud and Gay, 1966.

Macho-Diez, A. *Targum Palestinense: MS de la Biblioteca Vaticana, Tome I: Genesis.* Madrid: CSIC, 1968.

Mann, J. *The Bible as Read and Preached in the Old Synagogue.* Cincinnati: Hebrew Union College, 1940.

Meyer, H. *Kritisch exegetisches Handbuch uber den Brief an die Galater.* Göttingen: Vandenhoeck und Ruprecht, 1886.

Miller, Merrill P. "Targum, Midrash and the Use of the Old Testament in the New Testatment," *JJS* 2 (1971) 29-82.

_____ "Midrash" in *IDBSup* Nashville: Abingdon, 1976. 593-597.

Myers, Jacob. *I and II Esdras.* Garden City: Doubleday, 1974.

Neff, R. W. "The Pattern of Annunciation in the Birth Narratives of the O.T." Unpublished dissertation, Yale University, 1969.

_____ "The Birth and Election of Isaac in the Priestly Tradition," *Biblical Research* 15 (1970) 5-18.

Neher, Andre. "Le symbolisme conjugal: expression de l'histoire dans l'ancien testament," *RHPR* 34 (1954) 30-49.

Neumann, Eric. *The Great Mother.* Princeton: University Press, 1963.

Nielsen, P. "Die altesemitische Muttergottin," *ZDMG* 92 (1938) 504-551.

North, C. R. *The Second Isaiah.* Oxford: Clarendon, 1964.

Noth, Martin. *Die Israelite Personannamen im Rahmen der Gemeinsemitischen Namengebung.* Stuttgart: Kohlhammer, 1928.

xxxxxxxxxx. *History of the Pentateuchal Traditions.* Englewood Cliffs: Prentice Hall, 1972.

Parker, Simon. "The Marriage Blessing in Israelite and Ugaritic Literature," *JBL* 95 (1976) 23-30.

Patai, Raphael. *The Hebrew Goddess.* New York: Ktav, 1967.

Patte, Daniel. *Early Jewish Hermeneutic in Palestine.* Missoula: Scholars, 1975.

Perrot. C. "Les récits d'enfance dans la haggadah," *RSR* 55 (1967) 481-518.

Pfeiffer, Robert. "Midrash in the Books of Samuel." In *Quantulacumque*, ed. Casey, Lake and Lake. London: Christophers, 1937.

Philo, *Treatises*, in ten volumes, trans. F. H. Colson and G. H. Whitaker; Loeb Classical Library. Cambridge: Harvard, 1971.

Porteous, Norman W. "Jerusalem-Zion: The Growth of a Symbol." In *Verbannung und Heimkehr*, ed. Kuschke. Tübingen: J. C. B. Mohr, 1961.

Press, R. "Der Prophet Samuel," *ZAW* 36 (1938) 177-225.

Pritchard, James B. *Palestinian Figurines in Relation to Certain Goddesses Known Through Literature*. New Haven: American Oriental Society, 1943.

_____ *The Ancient Near East in Pictures Relating to the Old Testament*. Princeton: University Press, 1959.

_____ *The Bronze Age Cemetery at Gibeon*. Philadelphia: University of Pennsylvania Museum, 1963.

_____ *The Ancient Near East: Supplementary Texts and Pictures Relating to the Old Testament*. Princeton: University Press, 1965.

_____ *Ancient Near Eastern Texts*. Princeton: University Press, 1969.

Quell, G. "Das Phänomen des Wunders im Alten Testament." In *Verbannung und Heimkehr*, ed. A. Kuschke. Tübingen: J. C. B. Mohr, 1961.

Reik, Theodore. *The Creation of Woman*. New York: McGraw-Hill, 1960.

Richter, Wolfgang. *Traditionsgeschichtliche Untersuchungen zum Richterbuch*. Bonn: Peter Hanstein, 1963.

Rollenbleck, E. *Magna Mater im A.T.* Darmstadt: Claassen and Roether, 1949.

Sanders, James A. "Dissenting Deities and Philippians 2:1-11," *JBL* 88 (1969) 279-90.

_____ *The Dead Sea Psalms Scroll*. Ithaca: Cornell, 1971.

_____ *Torah and Canon*. Philadelphia: Fortress, 1971, ^{2}1974, ^{3}1976.

_____ "The Ethic of Election in Luke's Great Banquet Parable." In *Essays in Old Testament Ethics (J. Philip Hyatt, In Memoriam)*, ed. James L. Crenshaw and John T. Willis. Ne York: Ktav, 1974.

_____ "From Isaiah 61 to Luke 4," *Christianity, Judaism and Other Greco-Roman Cults.* In *Studues for Morton Smith at Sixty,* ed. Jacob Neusner. Leiden: Brill, 1975, Part I.

_____ "Torah and Christ," *Int* 29 (1975) 372-90.

_____ "Adaptable for Life: The Nature and Function of Canon." In *Magnalia Dei: The Mighty Acts of God. Essays on the Bible and Archaeology in Memory of G. Ernest Wright,* ed. F. M. Cross, W. E. Lemke and P. D. Miller. Garden City: Doubleday, 1976.

_____ "Hermeneutics in True and False Prophecy." In *Canon and Authority,* ed. George E. Coats and Burke O. Long. Philadelphia: Fortress, 1977.

_____ "Torah and Paul." In *God's Christ and His People,* ed. Wayne Meeks. Oslo: Universitatsforlaget, 1977.

_____ "Biblical Criticism and the Bible as Canon," *USQR* 32 (1977) 157-165.

_____ Articles on "Hermeneutics" and "Torah," *IDBSup* Nashville: Abingdon, 1976. 402-07, 909-11.

Schafers, J. "I Sam. 1-15: Literarkritisch Untersucht," *BZ* 5 (1907) 1-21.

Schlier, H. *Der Brief an die Galater.* Göttingen: Vandenhoeck und Ruprecht, 1965.

Schmidt, K. L. "Jerusalem als Urbild und Abbild," *Eranos-Jahrbuch* 18 (1950) 207-248.

Schülte, Hannelis. *Die Entstehung der Geschichtsschreibung im Alten Israel.* Berlin: de Gruyter, 1972.

Schüpphaus, Joachim. *Richter und Prophetengeschichten als Glieder der Geschichtsdarstellung der Richter-und Königszeit.* Bonn: Rheinischen Friedrich-Wilhelms-Universität, 1967.

Seeligmann, I. C. *The Septuagint Version of Isaiah.* Leiden: Brill, 1948.

Skinner, John. *Genesis.* Edinburgh: Clark, 1910.

Smith, Morton. *Palestinian Parties and Politics that Shaped the Old Testament.* New York: Columbia University Press, 1971.

Sperber, A. *The Bible in Aramaic.* Leiden: Brill, 1957-62. Four volumes.

Stenning, J. F. *The Targum of Isaiah.* Oxford: Clarendon, 1948.

Stoebe, H. J. *Das Erste Buch Samuelis.* Gütersloh: Mohn, 1973.

Terrien, Samuel. "The Omphalos Myth and Hebrew Religion," *VT* 20 (1970) 135-338.

_____ "Toward A Biblical Theology of Womanhood," *Religion in Life* 42 (1973) 322-333.

Theodor, J. and C. Albech. *Midrash Bereshit Rabba*. Jerusalem: Wahrmann, 1965.

Torrey, C. C. *The Second Isaiah*. New York: Scribner, 1928.

Tov, E. *The Book of Baruch*. Missoula: Scholars, 1975.

Towner, Wayne S. *The Rabbinic "Enumeration of Scriptural Examples."* Leiden: Brill, 1973.

Trible, Phyllis. "Depatriarchalizing in Biblical Interpretation," *JAAR* 41 (1973) 30-48.

van der Berghe, P. "Ani et Anaw dans les Psaumes." In *Le Psautier*, ed. R. DeLanghe. Louvain: Publications Universitaires, 1962.

van Seters, John. *Abraham in History and Tradition*. New Haven: Yale University, 1975.

_____ "The Problem of Childlessness in Near Eastern Law and the Patriarchs of Israel," *JBL* 87 (1968) 401-408.

Volz, Paul. *Jesaia* II. Leipzig: Scholl, 1932.

_____ *Die Eschatologie der jüdischen Gemeinde*. Tübingen: J. C. B. Mohr, 1934.

von Rad, Gerhard. *Genesis*. Philadelphia: Westminster, 1961.

Wellhausen, Julius. *Der Text der Bücher Samuelis*. Göttingen: Vandenhoeck und Ruprecht, 1871.

Westermann, Claus. *Isaiah 40-66*. Philadelphia: Westminster, 1969.

Whybray, R. N. *Wisdom in Proverbs*. London: SCM, 1965.

Wildberger, H. *Jesaja*. Neukirchen-Vluyn: Neukirchener, 1972.

Wiseman, D. J. *The Vassal-Treaties of Esarhaddon*. London: British School of Archeology in Iraq, 1958.

Yonge, C. D. *The Works of Philo Judaeus*. London: Bohn, 1854.

Index

Genesis

Reference	Pages
11:28-30	20
11:30	17-21, 67, 118, 120
12:10-20	110
12:28-30	20
14:19	118
15:1-3	17
16	21-23, 28-29, 42, 99, 107, 111
16:1	28, 29
16:2	29, 96, 127, 133
16:3	29
16:5	29
16:1-6	29
16:12	21
16:17-18	17
18:1-15	17
18:1	18
18:2	18
18:10	18, 20
18:11	96-97
18:13-14	18
18:14	106
18:22-33	129
20:17	124
20:18	132
21	21-22
21:1	19, 96n., 124, 130, 133
21:1-6	17
21:6	96, 136
21:7	120, 122, 134
21:8-12	22
21:9-10	107
21:12	108
21:19	22
24:60	15, 126
25:13-16	25
25:18	21
25:19-26	30
25:20	30
25:21	17, 30, 67, 118, 121, 126, 139
25:21-28	30n.
25:26	30
28:14	70
29:31	67, 118, 121, 131
29:31-30:24	17, 23-29
30	28, 42
30:1-4	29
30:1-24	22, 23
30:1	28, 41, 67
30:3	29
30:4	29
30:5	29
30:11	122
30:17	139
30:29	121
30:20	121
30:22	118, 139
30:23	102
37:9	118
50:20	33

Exodus

Reference	Pages
2	41n.
20:11	119
22:16-17	68n.
23:26	15, 91n.

Leviticus

18:9	68n.
20:20-21	16
26	15
20:24	118

Numbers

6:1-21	338n.
14:36	47
21:5	47
21:25	65

Deuteronomy

7:14	15, 30n. 91n.
12:12	43
14:26	43
15:20	43
16:11	43
22:28-29	68n.
23:21	92n.
25:5-10	16
25:21	16
28:1-4	15
32	46, 52-53
32:18	61

Judges

13	17, 36-37, 116n.
13:2	36-37, 67
13:3	67, 121
13:4	37
13:5	37
13:7	37
13:14	37
16:4	119
16:21	119

Ruth

4:11-12	14

1 Samuel

1	32, 36, 41, 46-47, 55, 100 116n.
1-2	17, 52n., 53, 55, 127
1-3	35-36, 40-42, 47, 55-59, 63, 137
1:2	37, 122
1:3	42
1:4-8	42, 51
1:4-9	44
1:5	45
1:5-6	43, 45-46, 51
1:6	47, 51, 52n.
1:6-7	55
1:6-8	47
1:7	43-47, 51
1:8	51
1:9	43
1:11	37, 50-51, 102, 118-119, 127
1:12-13	50, 129
1:12-18	50
1:15	37
1:15-16	50
1:16	45-46, 51
1:20	36
1:21	42
1:2	36, 37
2:1-10	52-53, 55
2:1-11	51
2:5	54
2:6	104
2:8	104-105
2:9	54
2:11-26	55
2:19	42
2:20	36-37
2:21	37, 121-122, 127
2:22	53
2:35	53
2:36	53
3	40, 55
7:3-4	40
7:3-17	339
7:6	39
7:15-17	39
7:16-17	118-119
8:1	39
8:10-18	40
9	39-40
12:6-18	40
12:11	39
14:1	43n.
15:2	133

Index

2 Samuel

13:19-20	68
20:19	65
22:1-23:7	52

2 Kings

4	19, 135
4:8-17	17, 19n.
4:8	43n.
4:16	20
18:4	80n.
21:1-9	80n.
23:6	80n.

1 Chronicles

4:3	119

2 Chronicles

5:2	7

Ezra

10:1-44	77

Nehemiah

13:23-30	77

Job

1:6	43n.
18:19	16

Psalms

6:7-8	46
9:13-14	50
10:12	50
31:11	47
31:10-12	46
42:4-5	51
42:11	51
44:25	50
55:3	51
64:2	51
96:34	131
74:19	50
78:58	48
83:7	22
99:6	40n.
102:1	51
104:34	46n.
107:33-34	91
113:9	120-121, 134
132:14	119-120
142:3	51
145:14	32
145:19	127

Proverbs

1-9	75, 82
8:22-31	75, 76
30:16	16, 91

Song of Songs

2:14	126

Isaiah

1:21	66n.
12:1	79
14:22	16
40:1	79
44:23	67
47:1	65
49:8	68
49:13	67, 79
49:19	68, 122
49:19-21	59, 64, 78
49:21	121
49:22-23	78
51:1	65
51:1-3	59, 64n.
51:2	60-61, 65, 67
51:3	61, 79
51:4	64
51:4-10	64n.
51:9-11	62
51:12	79
52:9	79
52:11-12	9
54:1	67, 98-99, 107, 111, 116, 118-119, 120, 121-122
54:1-3	59, 62-63, 65, 67, 78

54:2	72	**Malachi**	
54:2-3	69		
55:1-2	78-79	4:5-6	101
56:4	93		
65:4-5	92	**Matthew**	
57:18	79		
58:14	78	1	116n.
59:20	122	26:41	108
61:4	68		
62:4	68	**Mark**	
66:7-14	77		
66:9	78	14:38	108
66:10-11	79		
66:10-12	78	**Luke**	
66:10-14	135		
66:11	77, 79	1-2	100-107, 116n.
		1:6	100
Jeremiah		1:7	100
		1:25	102
2:27	61	1:28-31	106
15:1	40n.	1:35	103
30:17	122	1:37	106
31:15	81-82	1:67-69	100
31:15	24, 86-87, 112	3:15-18	101
		4	2n., 11
Ezekiel		11:1-3	129
		14	11
16	7, 66n.	22:28, 40	
17:24	132	46	108
23	66n.		
27:35	47	**John**	
33:10	6n, 62		
33:23-30	72	5:39	9
37:1-11	103		
		Acts	
Hosea			
		2:24	104, 105
2:1	66		
9:10-18	16	**Romans**	
9:11-14	91		
		1:3-4	103
Zephaniah		4:16-17	109
		9:6-9	108
3:14-17	106		
		Galatians	
Zechariah			
		4:2	109
9-11	90n.	4:21-31	107-113, 105n.
		4:26	141

Index

Philippians

2:1-11	11
2:8	104

Revelation

12	141
21	79n., 114n., 141

www.ingramcontent.com/pod-product-compliance
Lightning Source LLC
Chambersburg PA
CBHW022012160426
43197CB00007B/391